Belize

Ecotourism in action

Second Edition

Meb Cutlack

D1527029

CARIBBEAN

First edition 1993
Second edition 2000
Published by MACMILLAN EDUCATION LTD
London and Oxford
Companies and representatives througout the world

www.macmillan-caribbean.com

ISBN 0–333–77329–2

10	9	8	7	6	5	4	3	2	1
09	08	07	06	05	04	03	02	01	00

This book is printed on paper suitable for recycling and
made from fully managed and sustained forest sources.

Printed in Malaysia

A catalogue record for this book is available from the
British Library.

Acknowledgements

The author and publishers wish to thank the National Geographic Society for permission
to quote from the Introduction to the article 'La Ruta Maya' by Wilbur E. Garrett,
October, 1989.

The publishers have made every effort to trace the copyright holders, but if they have
inadvertently overlooked any, they will be pleased to make the necessary arrangements at
the first opportunity.

Front cover photograph Keel-billed toucan (NHPA/Martin Harvey)
Back cover photograph Xunantunich (N. Gillard)

Contents

1	Historical background	1
2	The climate and geography	13
3	The people of Belize	18
4	The economy	26
5	The environment	35
6	Belize City, Belmopan and the district towns	37
7	The six districts	50
8	The Maya	62
9	Wildlife	70
10	Belize's wondrous underwater world	79
11	A guide to hotels, restaurants and shopping	83
12	General information	97

| 1 |
Historical background

Interpretations of the origin of the name Belize are nearly as varied as its ethnic groups. 'Belikin' is Mayan for 'road-to-the-east', whereas 'Beliz' means 'muddy-waters', an apt description of the Belize River during the rainy season. Some say that it is a corruption of the name Wallace, after Peter Wallace the pirate, an early arrival and coastal explorer in Belize. On the other hand, the French word 'balise' means 'beacon', a nautical term which might have had privateer-appeal. In Spanish, 'bella-isla', meaning 'beautiful island', is not so far-fetched a possibility as to be dismissible, considering Belize's numerous, gorgeous coral isles. And so it goes on .... In any event, despite this ambiguity, British Honduras officially changed its name to Belize in June 1973.

The how and why of Belize can, to some extent, be explained by her geography. There are jungle mountains and exposed plains in the interior, and swamp along a coastline guarded its entire length by the Barrier Reef which acts as a wall blocking the approach of all but the most intrepid. Navigators feared it, ships' captains avoided it, and only a rough group of men of many nationalities – Belize's legendary pirates and privateers – used it as a hideout from which to make forays into the shipping lanes beyond. It was a place to which they could flee with their booty but into which few navy frigates or merchant ships, even if well-armed, would dare follow. In the Belizean people today there is still alive an element of the freebooters of old, a pride, a reluctance to serve any man by order. Add to this an innate, easy-going friendliness and the unusual combination is disarming, to say the least.

Even today there are not many who approach Belize by sea. Visitors who are not arriving by air come by way of three border stations, and intruders – illegal immigrants, mostly from Central America – by way of the unpatrolled, unmarked expanse in between.

In some ways, Belize is an anachronism, a nineteenth century way of life somnambulating its way through the present. There are verandahed colonial houses straight out of Somerset Maughan; lobster sells locally at $12.00 a pound; seventy per cent of the

1

A fine example of Belize City architecture (M J BOURNE)

country is covered in forest, jungle and swamp in which an amazing diversity of creatures dwell – including the jaguar, the tapir, the howler monkey, the harpy eagle and the crocodile.

Belize's population of approximately 230,000 people inhabits the remainder of its 8,867 square miles (22,963 square kilometres) of land which, at the height of the ancient Mayan empire, supported a million or more. The country's projected population by the year 2000 is 241,492, at the present growth rate of 2.6 per cent. With its British educational and legal systems still intact, this English-speaking enclave sits serenely amidst its temperamental Latin neighbours despite the fact that it is comprised of minorities from around the world who have settled here over centuries. There are descendants of pirates, logwood cutters and slaves; Mayans who never left, Mayans who came back, and Mayans intermingled with the Spanish conquistadors whose descendants are called Mestizos; Garifuna from Africa via St Vincent and the Mosquito Coast; Creoles from the Caribbean and Africa; Lebanese, Chinese, East Indians, Britons, Mennonites and North Americans. Racial lines are often blurred, with dabs of different colours in almost everyone.

Unlike almost any other people on the face of the earth, Belizeans have known no real masters other than themselves, for the Maya did in fact keep Mayan slaves. However, while their kinsmen to the north, west and south fell to the dominion of the conquistadors, the Mayans in Belize for the most part disappeared into the jungles, and returned when the coast was clear. At Tipu in the Cayo District, indications are that Christian 'conversion' by Spanish missionaries was soon followed by subversion, for Mayan fetishes have been found buried within the church. Belize's early settlers from Mexico were on the run from harsh rule (the War of the Castes) in which the Mestizos were persecuted by both the Mayans and the Spanish. Of course the European buccaneers knew only the cruel rule of 'an eye for an eye', which no doubt accounts for the tradition of the seemingly inevitable eye patches. However, when they turned their attention to plundering the logwood and mahogany trees of the pristine forests, their fierce independence became a communal matter and translated into a surprisingly democratic system of self-rule, with only overtones of British colonialism. Even their black slaves, bought in the Caribbean markets to do the actual wood-cutting, could stand with axe or machete in hand and stare any overseer straight in the eye. Survival was the real rule, and all obeyed it.

History has often dropped upon the shores of Belize the flotsam and jetsam of other countries' conflicts: runaway planters and landowners from the south of the United States (as the 1861–1865 Civil War denied them the slave system and its economy, they thought to reinstate their former way of life in Belize); European army deserters; escapees from South American revolutions; and gold seekers gone astray. Ironically, none of them changed Belize, but Belize did change them. Slavery had been abolished in Belize in 1838, and soon the new citizens were having their say at town meetings, although few could meet the property requirements necessary to establish the right to vote. It was not until 1954 that universal suffrage came into being.

Having always been free, Belize did not get around to establishing independence from Britain until 1981. Virtual self-government had been in force since 1964, and actual independence was achieved on 21 September, 1981. Belize became a member of the Commonwealth, and also of the United Nations and the Non-Aligned Movement. She had to wait until 1991 to be admitted to the Organization of American States. Until 1993, Belize had 2,000 British troops billeted on her soil at her own request, to protect her from a spurious territorial claim by Guatemala. Now there are only two hundred. They are referred to as the British Army Training Support Unit – Belize. The Belize Defence Force (BDF) is the first line of defence against any external attack and is also active in other national security operations. The BDF has a full-time force of 1,500 men and women. There is also a National Reserve Force. There are sporadic military exercises in Belize which include Belizean, British, Dutch and US Forces, yet for nearly two hundred years no great conflict nor war has touched the people or country of Belize.

Early times

A slice across Belizean life 1,500 years ago would have shown a prosperous Mayan society, consisting of city states of ten to twenty thousand inhabitants with a peripheral agricultural industry, trading in cacao beans, fish, shells, obsidian, jade, copper and pottery from other Mayan areas along the coast and up along Belize's many rivers. At cities such as Caracol, Cahal Pech, El Pilar and Altun Ha, the famous Mayan ball courts provided the venue for important ceremonies and entertainment. That the winners sometimes lost their heads – literally – no doubt added extra spice. Priests held powerful sway over daily and religious life from their lofty temple pyramids which dominate all towns of any size. Warfare between neighbouring city states was the business of civil power, much as in feudal Europe where neighbourhood sieges decided local dominance. It is known that in AD 562 a major battle took place between Caracol in western Belize and Tikal, about sixty miles away in Guatemala, and that Caracol emerged victorious.

The seventeenth century was the time when the pirates began to prey on shipping in the Caribbean area. Huge shipments of gold and precious stones from South America, Panama and Mexico, the spoils of invasion, were heading towards Spain and the Old World. The pirates used Belize as their base of operation to prey upon the pillagers, with river mouths and mangrove creeks serving as sanctuaries in the unlikely event that those in foolish pursuit had somehow managed to evade calamity on the coral heads and sand bars. To this day there is many a legend of fabulous treasure from the secret hoards of the pirates. The *Field Guide to Ambergris Caye,* by R.L. Woods, S. Tomlinson-Reid and A.M. Reid, relates one of these tales:

19

*On the main coast of Belize, there is a rocky promontory named
Little Rocky Point. In the '60s a Chilean came to Ambergris Caye
and purchased a large tract of beach-front property north of Tres
Cocos (now the Peter Handcock property). Despite his land
holdings on Ambergris Caye, his attention seemed to be focused
on Little Rocky Point on the mainland. He hired quite a few
residents of San Pedro to help with excavations in the Little
Rocky Point area. One day all of the workers were laid off and
apparently the Chilean went back to Little Rocky Point. He then
returned to Ambergris Caye, and about that time a Mexican
gunboat appeared off the Caye. Both gunboat and the Chilean
then left the island. Speculation has it that the Chilean had a
treasure map of some kind, and may have recovered a
substantial treasure that he spirited elsewhere.*

This report coincides in many respects with a tale told by a
resident of the Little Rocky Point area. He related how in the 1960s
a stranger, who seemed to be Spanish, appeared 'with a big yacht
and a lot of workers'. They employed a local man and his family to
help them dig in an area near the river. Eventually the Spaniard paid
the man to take his wife on holiday and, when the man returned, the
stranger, the yacht and all the other men had gone. However, on the
doorstep was a small package containing a quantity of gold valued at
that time at about $1,000. Of such stuff are the many treasure tales
of Belize.

However, more mundane affairs were already occupying most
Belizeans in the late seventeenth and eighteenth centuries.
Logwood cutting started up and soon became an important trade,
the logs being cut and shipped to Europe for their then valuable
purple dye. The British were the mainstay of this trade in timber and
this continued when mahogany came into its own. Although Spain
laid claim to Belizean territory, and attempted to expel the Baymen
(the earliest settlers) on several occasions during the first half of the
eighteenth century, she never actually made settlements. Meanwhile,
the Baymen, having established a community and a viable industry,
sought the protection of the British and were put under the
guardianship of Jamaica. In 1773 the British signed the Treaty of
Paris with the Spanish, giving the Baymen logwood rights within
specified areas; this area was extended by the Treaty of Versailles in
1783, and the Convention of London of 1786 which permitted

5

Many artifacts have been found in the excavations of Mayan temples and dwellings
(JACK PHILLIPS)

mahogany cutting as well. Nonetheless, the Baymen persisted in exceeding their rights, which eventually led to the Battle of St George's Caye in 1798 when the Spanish attacked this offshore island with a flotilla of thirty-two ships and a large but reluctant force of men. HMS *Merlin*, together with a small makeshift naval defence manned by Baymen and their slaves, managed to repulse the Spanish invasion. This victory is celebrated as a national holiday on 10 September.

The early 1800s were a time of consolidation for Belize's mahogany trade. It became the lifeblood of the nation, providing the rich and influential of England, Europe and the United States with the raw material for furniture of drawing room, bedroom and dining room. While some furniture was made in Belize, the amount was negligible compared to the thousands of tons of mahogany logs, sawn rough board and rosewood logs exported to Jamaica. Men owning the timber concessions could be taxed twice if they produced furniture for export in Belize, a colonial legality which stopped the young country from establishing what could have been an important industry. This, and the English administrative policy to discourage agriculture in order to keep the people dependent on Britain, have had repercussions which reverberate in Belize to this day.

Timber cutting in the Mountain Pine Ridge (RICHARD HUNT)

7

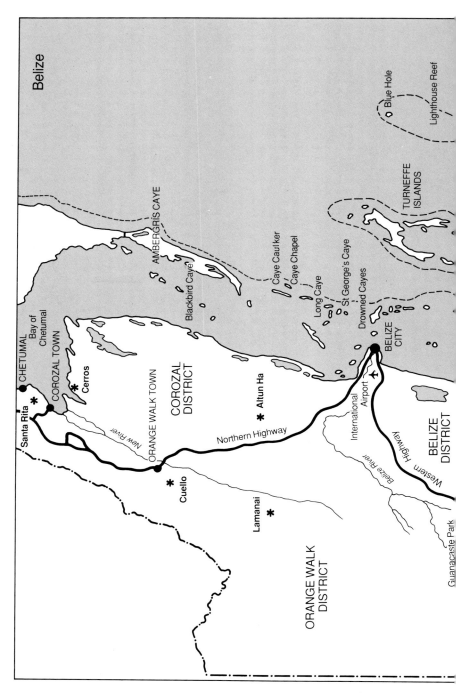

Belize

Blue Hole
Lighthouse Reef

TURNEFFE
ISLANDS

AMBERGRIS CAYE

Blackbird Caye

Caye Caulker
Caye Chapel

Long Caye

St George's Caye

Drowned Cayes

BELIZE
CITY

CHETUMAL
Bay of
Chetumal

COROZAL TOWN

Cerros

Santa Rita

ORANGE WALK TOWN

COROZAL
DISTRICT

New River

* Altun Ha

Northern Highway

International
Airport

Belize River

Western Highway

BELIZE
DISTRICT

* Cuello

* Lamanai

ORANGE WALK
DISTRICT

Guanacaste Park

8

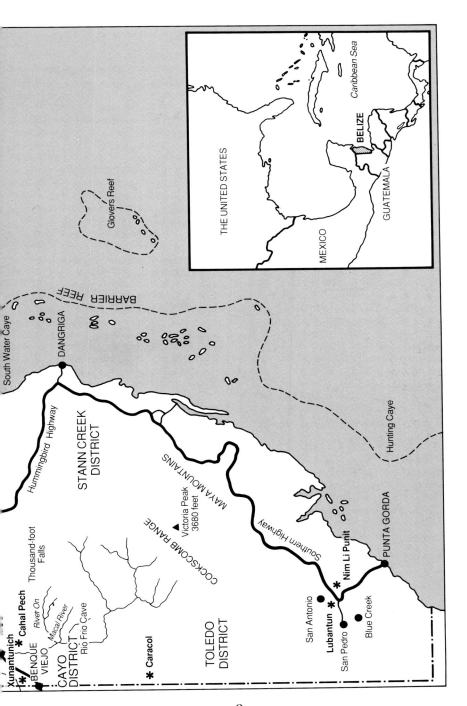

THE UNITED STATES

MEXICO

Caribbean Sea

BELIZE

GUATEMALA

Glovers Reef

South Water Caye

BARRIER REEF

DANGRIGA

Hunting Caye

STANN CREEK DISTRICT

Hummingbird Highway

MAYA MOUNTAINS

Victoria Peak
3680 feet

COCKSCOMB RANGE

Thousand-foot
Falls

River On

Macal River

Rio Frio Cave

Southern Highway

Nim Li Punit

PUNTA GORDA

San Antonio

Lubantun

San Pedro

Blue Creek

TOLEDO DISTRICT

Xunantunich

Cahal Pech

BENQUE
VIEJO

CAYO
DISTRICT

* Caracol

9

Because of the Baymen's dependency on slaves as a source of manpower at a time when Payo Obispo, just across the Rio Hondo in Mexico, was offering freedom to those who escaped; and because Belizean slaves wielded power in the form of the axes they used for cutting down trees, as well as outnumbering their 'masters', the African-Belizeans were already somewhat integrated into society by the time of emancipation in 1838. Racial admixtures were already in obvious evidence. In 1839 an American explorer, John L. Stephens, passed through Belize and wrote the following description of his visit to Belize City:

On my way back I stopped at the house of a merchant, whom I found at what is called a second breakfast. The gentleman sat on one side of the table and his lady on the other. At the head was a British officer, and opposite him a mulatto. By chance a place was made for me between the two coloured gentlemen. Some of my countrymen, perhaps, would have hesitated about taking it, but I did not; both were well dressed, well educated, and polite. They talked of their Mahogany works, of England, hunting horses, ladies and wine; and before I had been an hour in Belize I learned that the great work of controversy at home had been going on quietly for generations; that colour was considered mere matter of taste; and that some of the most respectable inhabitants had black wives and mongrel children, whom they educated with as much care, and made money for with as much zeal, as if their kids were perfectly white.

The British influence in Belize remained strong enough for a large contingent of Belizean men to be sent to Europe to fight, not only in the First World War, but again in the Second World War. In the first instance Belizean blacks and coloureds received a very rude shock indeed. Although Belize was by no means a society totally free of racial prejudice, its attitude was light years ahead of others in the Commonwealth. Belize's troops travelling overseas encountered the harsh reality of the black position in the outside world: an inferior social status and unashamed prejudice against them. Quite reasonably they did not like it and, as the war came to an end and Belize's troops came home, they brought with them a distrust of white Europeans and Americans. The lesson was reinforced in the Second World War and a degree of reservation still remains today. It goes a long way to explaining why Belizeans are reluctant, having

Government House, Belize City (M J BOURNE)

gained their sovereignty, ever to relinquish an iota of it to anyone, at any price, and that includes the many high-powered investors who come knocking at Belize's door hoping to conclude megadeals. One such was a famed German globetrotter, an investor, who ended up pouring billions of dollars into Brazil in a paper pulp and forestry scheme. His first choice was Belize, but the then government looked over his proposals and saw not only that he wanted a large chunk of Belize, but also that he proposed acting outside the normal laws of the land. They answered him with a resounding 'no'.

Between the wars, Belize discovered a new industry by producing and delivering rum for an America whose thirst was wetted rather than dampened by Prohibition. Many of today's store and warehouse fronts along the Belize City river entrance bear witness to how lucrative the trade was. Belize became a major stock and purchase centre for Caribbean rum runners, both offshore and inshore.

Despite the bad news of racialism abroad, young Belizeans returning home from the Second World War brought back new and progressive ideas of labour's dignity, the need to unionise and to create a new political era for Belize. Out of these yearnings sprang the Belize political parties of today – both the People's United Party

11

21 September, Independence Day celebrations (RICHARD HUNT)

and United Democratic Party. Ironically, in moulding labour into a political force, union power that might have achieved a prominent position was eclipsed. Today the unions, while truly representative of workers in different fields, still do not wield the enormous influence that they do in some other Caribbean countries, nor do they have the power that unions once traditionally held in Britain.

A cross-section of Belizean life in the post-Second World War era would show a young country with undercurrents of nationalism and independence beginning to emerge, but cut off from the mainstream development happening in the USA and Europe; a country only slowly awakening under the lightweight but dull blanket of colonial rule, with few real ideas of how to get out from under the blanket without being swaddled up in a similar blanket of US interests.

12

| 2 |
The climate and geography

Belize lies in the temperate sub-tropics with Mexico to the north and Guatemala to the west and south. In the Caribbean Sea to the east lie her own lovely islands, spilling down the entire length of her coastline like a jade necklace come unstrung. The thermometer rarely falls below 60°F, and almost never rises above 95°F, the median being 73–88°F. Within its small area, it contains a stunning variety of flora and fauna and much geographic diversity. It is a land of jungle-clad mountains, navigable rivers meandering endless miles, natural forests, open savannah plains, swamp lands and lagoons that dwarf the Everglades, plus hundreds of offshore cayes, two major atolls, and a bountiful Barrier Reef equalled by none in the northern hemisphere and second only to Australia's Great Barrier Reef.

Hidden Valley, in the Cayo District, shows some of the diversity of the Belize landscape (RICHARD HUNT)

The Rio Frio Cave (RICHARD HUNT)

Scenically the country is a wonderland, an untouched wilderness which the overzealous twentieth century has left alone, as much a demographic oddity among her crowded Central American neighbours as she is a cultural perplexity with her English language and manners amidst Latin surroundings. It is this paucity of population which has kept Belize almost unspoilt to this day, allowing hundreds of square miles of forest, savannah, wetlands and cayes to remain intact, free from pesticides and pollutants, so that many secrets remain hidden, even in her soil, and in the plant and animal life which thrives in the rare privacy of nature.

Traditionally there is the rainy season, the dry season and the 'little dry' – also called the 'mah-gray' (meagre, maugre) – of August. However, none of this projection of weather on to particular months can be depended upon, because every year tells a different story. The surest gauge to Belize's weather patterns is how far south Canadian weather comes in the 'winter', and how the tropical conversion belt affects Belize in the 'summer'. Take a wild winter storm that descends from Canada as far south as Texas, leaving snowdrifts

The town of San Pedro on Ambergris Caye from the air (opposite) (RICHARD HUNT)

14

down the Rockies and frozen water pipes throughout the Midwest of the USA. Belize will feel the tail end of it and have some rain and maybe a temperature drop down to the 60s °F. In the summer, take a tropical wave that moves across the Atlantic, continues up through the Caribbean and batters the US coast even as far north as Cape Cod. Belize will have storm force winds and rain and temperatures in the 70s °F. Round about September, that same tropical wave, if it has originated east of the 60°W longitude, may veer directly into Belize. The last hurricane to cause massive loss of life was Hattie, in 1961, in which 275 people perished. Largely because of this, plans were made to move the capital from Belize City, with its vulnerable coastal location, to an inland situation. These plans became reality in 1971 with the establishment of Belmopan, placed practically in the exact centre of the country. The only hurricane since Hattie, called Greta, caused quite a bit of damage to property in 1978. Today, a greater understanding of weather patterns allows much greater predictability and, therefore, warning.

Here is a rough guide to weather patterns in Belize:

October to May: Mostly fair weather with trade winds, some intermittent rain, temperature normally 73°F to 88°F with occasional drops to the 60s °F.

May to July: Heavy rains some years but not others, temperatures normal.

July to Sept: Sometimes very heavy rains, sometimes not, rarely lasting for more than one day at a time; temperatures slightly higher than in winter.

This weather pattern holds for Belize as a whole, but rain patterns differ markedly from one end of the country to the other, which also accounts for the contrast in vegetation. As a general rule, the further south you go the more rain you encounter. The northern half of Belize receives 60 to 80 inches per annum, the lower middle section perhaps 100 to 120 inches per annum, and the deep south up to 180 inches per annum. These statistics tend to frighten tourists and investors away from the south, yet most of the rain falls at night; usually the mornings are crisp and clear and sunny, the afternoons remaining the same.

An aerial view of the Barrier Reef near Ambergris Caye (opposite) (RICHARD HUNT)

17

| 3 |
The people of Belize

**A group of friends from four of the ethnic groups found
in Belize: Mayan, Creole, Garifuna and Carib** (RICHARD HUNT)

The faces of Belize are those of a society made up of every racial and
ethnic group imaginable: dark and light and each shade in between,
beauty cast from African, American Indian, Chinese, Arab, Caucasian
and East Indian. Some are recent mixes, some date back to pirate
and logwood-cutting times when English and Irish and European
adventurers created new strains with Creole and Indian women;
others, particularly among the Maya and Garifuna and the more
recently arrived Mennonites, reflect bloodlines unchanged in
centuries.

In simplistic terms, Belize's majority ethnic group consists of
Creoles, originally from Africa, many by way of other Caribbean
island nations, and many also with the blood strains of Belize's early
settlers from Europe. This group, perhaps more than any other,
gives Belize its unique quality of friendship, warmth and wisdom
and also its independence of both body and spirit. This group's

superiority in numbers is being increasingly challenged by the country's second largest group – the Mestizos and Latinos, including those from the surrounding Latin republics and from Mexico. Such a threat, which many fear will change Belize from the present easygoing, peaceful and friendly country into a more 'macho' Latin culture, is recognised by the Government. Great importance is put on absorbing 'new' Belizeans from surrounding countries as quickly as possible into the Belizean culture with its emphasis on independence (innately and internationally), self-help, patriotism and, possibly above all, true democracy with a multi-party system of Government. In other words, Latin newcomers are encouraged to join in the way of life of the long-established Mestizo population of Belize.

Ironically, Mexico's Caste Wars of the early nineteenth century caused, at different times, both Mestizos and their Mayan enemies to flee to Belize for sanctuary. Many northern towns and villages in Belize were, in fact, established by one or another of these factions.

A Creole musician – Creole music is well represented
by Mr Peters' lively songs (CUBOLA ARCHIVES)

Mayan children get their water from a well (DERRICK HAMRICK)

Today people of Mestizo descent make up more than three-quarters of the population of northern Belize, and they play an important role in the nation's political, economic and social life. Belize's current Deputy Prime Minister, the Hon. John Briceño, is a Mestizo.

Belize's Maya retreated from the coastal areas of Belize under pressure from the logwood cutters in the mid-seventeenth century. Others that came from Guatemala to settle in Belize during the twentieth century live mostly in the south of the country. In the west, and in scattered villages in the north, are refugees from the Yucatan War of the Castes. Few are city dwellers, although nearly all now attend schools, vote and take an active part in the local political structure through their own Alcalde ('village elder') system, unchanged for centuries.

Belize is possibly unique in all of the Americas for the fact that its Mayan Indians are accorded exactly the same rights and privileges as all other Belizean citizens. There is no distinction of any sort, something which cannot be said of the surrounding republics, or South America, or indeed of the USA or Canada. Belize's former Deputy Prime Minister and now Minister of the Sugar Industry, Local Government and Latin American Affairs, the Hon. Florencio Marin, is a Mayan and one of Parliament's longest serving members. The Minister of Rural Development and Culture, the Hon. Marcial Mes, who holds post-graduate degrees is also a Mayan.

Dangriga, and the southern areas of Belize, have a large Garifuna population and here are found people who managed to keep their culture intact even when they were unceremoniously transported to the Mosquito Coast from the Caribbean island of St Vincent, where they had emerged from a co-mingling of ex-slaves and natives. At the time of emancipation in Belize (the 1830s), some left the strife of Honduras, heading north and settling in Dangriga and the southern part of this country. They are a musical and artistic people, and Dangriga has truly become a center of art and music. Here is the home of such artists as Pen Cayetano and Benjamin Nicolas, who produce fine paintings representing the Garifuna culture and the folk traditions which make it unique. In addition, Dangriga claims fame as the originator of 'Punta Rock'. The town, too, is home to the Warigabaga (butterfly) Dancers whose talented feet, even in tennis shoes, still remember their African heritage. In addition to art the Garifuna people have made important contributions to education and throughout the public sector. The Speaker of the House of Representatives is Ms Sylvia Flores – a Garifuna.

Thatching a roof the Mayan way (M K AND ROB PHILLIPS)

A walk down any street in any town in Belize quickly reveals the influence of three other segments of Belize's varied racial mix. The roots of India, Lebanon and China are easily detected in the names and faces of merchants, shop-owners and restaurateurs, self-made entrepreneurs, many of them descendants of laborers brought to Belize by the British in the early nineteenth century to build roads, canals and even railways, often making use of the logging tracks created for hauling mahogany and hardwoods, the remains of which can still be found in the bush.

The small, long-settled 'white' element in Belize, not counting the Mennonites, are a mixture of early English, Scottish and Irish families, some Germans, and post-Civil War Americans. These are families as proud of their 'Belizeanism' as the most patriotic of Creole, Garifuna or Mestizo families. While some have maintained their distinct 'white' roots by not marrying into any but 'white' families, most show distinct and healthy strains of ancestors who were not so single-minded. The present generations of these same families seem to have little inclination to retain their white snobbishness and, in fact, would probably now find it impossible. Belize's last racial barriers (and some existed in club memberships and suchlike into the middle half of the twentieth century) fell away with Independence in 1981. The barriers which remain are mostly economic and educational. The beauty of Belize is that its people, from whatever roots of however long – or short – ago, are Belizeans first, and whatever else second. It is thus a country of strong 'local' nationalism, and has been so as far back as 1796 when slave and freeman, merchant, woodcutter and even the local layabout combined their efforts to defeat a vastly superior attacking force of Spaniards. Ethnic elitism is inapplicable in a country in which a single family group is likely to contain a mixture of groups crossing not only racial lines but also those of religion, of 'class' and – perhaps even more indicative in this land of sports fans – of athletic teams!

Almost without exception, Belizeans share a desire to retain the established ethnic balance but there is a fear that it is fast being encroached upon by immigration into Belize from neighbouring Spanish-speaking countries. It is not only a fear of exchanging the democratic system of government and the elaborate but fair system

Fruit orchards near San Ignacio (previous page) (RICHARD HUNT)

24

of justice for the more arbitrary Latin approach to basic human rights, or a fear of undermining the old English system of land ownership and tenure which has endured for centuries. It is primarily a fear of losing that complex identity which calls itself Belize.

English is the official language of Belize, although Spanish, Garifuna, Kekchi or Mopan Maya, Chinese, or old German may be the first language spoken at home. Creole, a colourful re-interpretation of English, is the social language of the streets.

While the Maya and the Garifuna people are gradually moving out of their villages and into the mainstream of Belizean society, the Mennonites continue to stay very much in their own communities. They came to Belize during the 1950s, mostly from Canada and northern Mexico, having been given special permission from the then Belizean/British Government to be awarded tax concessions and exemptions from military service in accordance with the requirements of their religion. They were granted jungle lands to set up agricultural communities. Today a major share of Belize's agricultural produce comes from their farms. The Mennonites live in several different areas of Belize: Blue Creek and Shipyard in the north, Spanish Lookout and Barton Creek in the west, and small communities in the south.

Members of the 'colony', or the more rigidly traditional faction, (the Amish), still use iron wheels on their horse-drawn wagons for transportation which includes taking their produce to market. At the other extreme, the progressive Mennonites of Spanish Lookout use modern, mechanised farm equipment and drive their own trucks; a Mennonite from Blue Creek was the first person to be issued with a private aeroplane license in Belize! Because Mennonites rarely marry outside their communities, much less their society, there is serious risk of succeeding generations suffering degeneration through inbreeding. Hopefully, younger generation Mennonites are now beginning to see the results of this problem for themselves. Through its solution, they too may eventually become Belizeans-first.

| 4 |
The economy

Xunantunich – a major tourist attraction (N GILLARD)

Belize is a true land of milk and honey which, in the past, settled instead for sugar and wood. Between its mountains and lowlands, wide river valleys and forests, it is a land which can grow just about anything, and the Barrier Reef protects one of the world's most plentiful marine breeding grounds. At the same time, these natural attributes make Belize an ideal locale for what is becoming known as 'adventure' or 'eco' tourism. Having always 'had it all', as one American writer expressed it, Belize is only now beginning to recognise it!

In Mayan times, Belizean soil supported a population in excess of a million; it could easily do the same today. When the British first colonised the country they frightened most remaining Mayans back into the mountains and then actively discouraged all forms of agriculture, their motive being to focus attention on the cutting of

26

logwood and mahogany for export to the mills and factories of Jamaica and Britain. It meant that Belize remained a single product economy – timber – until years later when the world developed a sweet tooth and created another demand – sugar. This was brought to Belize from Yucatan by Mestizos fleeing the War of the Castes. Vast areas of the north and parts of the south were turned over to sugar production. This also suited the British but left Belize, like many other Caribbean countries, totally tied to the fluctuations of markets well out of reach.

The basis of Belize's economy remained unchanged in all but detail not just through the nineteenth century but also into and up to the middle of the twentieth. Only in the 1940s did the first changes emerge: the fish and lobster industries got under way, and honey, bananas, cacao, rice and livestock were given a start.

By the end of the Second World War the USA was gradually superseding the United Kingdom as a major trading partner for Belize. Interestingly enough, it is during these years that the Belizean fishing industry formed its strong and productive fishing co-operatives to protect Belizean fishermen against US giants monopolizing and buying very cheaply Belize's rich lobster crop.

Belize is an ideal location for the ecotourist (CUBOLA ARCHIVES)

27

Belize for many years had timber as its main export
(CUBOLA ARCHIVES)

Under the co-operatives the income from lobster grew rapidly and still today ranks high on the list of top export-earners for Belize. Unhappily, sugar was simultaneously being promoted as Belize's number one product. The sudden turnabout in the world sugar market and the US's sudden curtailing of many of its sugar quota buying agreements with Caribbean countries hit Belize hard. Almost overnight, what had been a vibrant industry teetered on the verge of collapse.

The short-sightedness of US policy on sugar quotas is best reflected by the fact that at the very time in the early 1980s that the US Administration decided to launch its all-out war on drugs throughout Central and South America, it cut its sugar quotas in these areas. The resultant drop in income for the cane farmers of northern Belize attracted them to an easier and more profitable cash crop – marijuana. The Belize Government today is still battling with this problem and showing signs of success both in redirecting farmers towards the lucrative winter vegetable market, and in showing farmers and smugglers alike that they mean business in their fight against drugs. This battle has intensified in recent years with the use of Belize as a through-route for cocaine from Colombia,

A turbulent sunset: tourism is now the growth industry in Belize
(CUBOLA ARCHIVES)

with huge cash rewards hard to match by legitimate enterprise. The United States Government continues to cooperate with the Belize Government in the war against the trafficking in illegal drugs. As a part of a regional programme, the US Administration provides equipment and training to the local security forces. It has also established a regional communications link with the US Drug Enforcement Agency.

It was not until a shift away from the policy of public ownership came in with the UDP (United Democratic Party) in 1984 that the important banana industry was finally set on the road to profit by privatization. The UDP also made tourism its second highest priority after agriculture, a trend continued and even accelerated when the PUP (People's United Party) regained power in 1989. These two changes in political attitude have encouraged rapid growth in the economy. Although, in order of importance in relation to dollar earnings, sugar is still number one, citrus, bananas, and tourism are steadily growing; and fishing, mostly lobster, conch and shrimp, but also grouper and snapper, is expanding fast. A new area of commercial interest is the inland farming of fish and shrimp, with shrimp farms now established near Belize City and in the mid-south.

29

Belize's growing handicraft industry, San Jose Succotz, Cayo District
(CUBOLA ARCHIVES)

These farms are expected to become big dollar earners for Belize in the future.

A relatively new idea in development for Belize is the manufacturing of clothing for export to US markets. There has been one major factory in Belize (Williamsons) for more than a decade but a number of new enterprises have now opened in Belize City, and in Corozal in the north. In some cases the clothing arrives ready-cut from its parent company in the US or the Far East, is sewn in Belize, and then exported – mostly to the US.

But sugar remains the number one industry and the main export earner. It accounted for BZ$91 million sales in 1997. (The Belize dollar is pegged to the US dollar, 2 to 1.) The banana industry accounted for BZ$52 million during the same period and citrus BZ$48 million. Earnings from fish and shrimp exports were BZ$35 million.

Tourism, as Belize's newest industry with the greatest international impact, deserves a closer look. It is the country's fastest growing sector and potentially her biggest winner, yet Belize has more to offer than long white sandy beaches. Belize offers

A typically beautiful beach at Caye Caulker (opposite)
(RICHARD HUNT)

Hiking in the Mountain Pine Ridge
(RICHARD HUNT)

snorkelling, diving on the reefs, fishing and sailing in the clear waters, and beachcombing on the many small, uninhabited islands and cayes. There are few traffic lights, much less the neon lights of glittering nightlife. Instead there are fireflies flicking on and off, giving emphasis to the real action going on in Belize: at Mayan temple sites hidden deep in the jungle where the jaguar stalks the paca, and parrots shriek the alarm.

This may not add up to every tourist's dream, but 'nature tourism' or 'ecotourism' is fast becoming a reality for more and more visitors every year. This is specialised travel which involves participation and a sense of adventure: horseback riding through jungle trails; paddling up – or inner-tubing down – beautiful rivers; exploring ancient Mayan ruins or spelunking in magical caves. It is all here for those with the gumption to go for it – and the willingness to pay good money for priceless memories.

At present there are just three or four live-aboard dive boats, and three cayes developed for general tourism, plus a handful more with their own island lodges. In the country itself, there is virtually no

**Windsurfing on the clear waters of Belize
off Ambergris Caye** (RICHARD HUNT)

luxury tourism infrastructure. Tourists should be reminded that the roads south are rough and that vehicles often reflect this abuse; however, the Southern Highway which links the Toledo District with the rest of the country is being improved and will soon be paved. The improvement of this southern route includes a plan to minimise the potential negative environmental, social and cultural impact on this region of the country.

Food is generally simple fare; and accommodation tends towards the basic, albeit clean, with running water, if only cold. Belize City itself has a few large, modern (and expensive) hotels plus several more modest hotels and guest houses, and the countryside boasts some charming lodges and a few good inns. In any event, the people are friendly and the water drinkable, as is the award-winning local beer, Belikin, and the excellent Belizean rums. It is simply a matter of not expecting Belize to be what it isn't – and appreciating what it is. To promote tourism the Government offers generous tax and import concessions and is going all-out to train and attract Belizeans into the industry.

Tourism in Belize started, as might be expected, out on the islands, in particular at Ambergris Caye and its fishing village of San Pedro. It was here that the first tourist hotels were built, the first tourist restaurants and bars were opened, and where the first barbecued lobster beach parties were held. Today it is Belize's most sophisticated tourism resort and yet it is still just an unassuming little town with sand streets where the local fishermen, as a sideline, guide tourists out to the reef. This is Belize. Today Belize lies poised on the brink of a dramatic new industry that could quickly raise living standards throughout the country and yet leave intact the country's unique natural features: its Mayan past, its exciting wildlife, its large areas of untouched rain forest, and its extraordinary Barrier Reef.

The Government, and especially the Ministries of Tourism and of Natural Resources and the Environment, are well aware of the potential of 'ecotourism' and are rapidly enhancing its prospects by creating new parks and reserves throughout the country. It is not tourism development in the sense of other Caribbean destinations, or of places like Cancun in Mexico, but the development of specialised tourism in the fields of archaeology, natural history, reef diving, and exploration in the unequalled waters between the reef and the mainland.

Belize's Barrier Reef, which is the largest in the Western World, was declared by UNESCO to be a World Heritage Site in 1997.

| 5 |

The environment

Belize remains unspoiled to a large extent because it was slow in getting on the development bandwagon which was taking place in the rest of the Caribbean and Central America – a process which showed little concern for the long-term effect of environmental damage. Because of this, the country is one of the regional leaders in environmental protection and now finds itself on the cutting-edge of a new demand in the tourism industry for nature or ecotourism.

With its marvellous Barrier Reef and coral islands, its richness in culture and temples of the ancient Maya, and the wonders of its rain forest, the country has been able to maintain its natural beauty; meanwhile investors and developers in the rest of the region were promoting mass tourism and building giant hotels at the expense of the environment.

Belize continues to offer a wide variety of tourist attractions within its relatively small land area, particularly to visitors interested in natural and cultural history. The country's low population density and extensive protected areas have resulted in some of the most intact marine and inland ecotourism attractions in the region. It has an impressive variety of Mayan ruins, as well as a diversity of cultures.

While there is not yet a clearly defined or fully implemented policy for the development of this industry, current practices clearly favor ecotourism over the traditional tourism development concepts seen in models around the rest of Central America and the Caribbean.

There is a strong tourism industry organization in the country – The Belize Tourism Industry Association (BTIA). They, along with environmental groups such as the Belize Audubon Society (BAS), advocate strongly for sustainable development which includes the cautious development of natural and cultural tourism in environmentally sensitive areas.

A significant portion of Belize is designated as national parks, sanctuaries or reserves or is otherwise locally protected. Under a mutual agreement with the Government of Belize, the Belize Audubon Society manages most of these protected areas. These include the Cockscomb Basin Wildlife Sanctuary which is the only jaguar reserve in this part of the world. The BAS manages these protected areas for the Government and people of Belize. It depends mainly on international support from foundations, private donors and international environmental groups to support its work. The Government has also passed a law (the PACT Act) which has led to the creation of a Protected Areas Conservation Trust for which some earnings from the tourism industry are used for environmental protection. While a defined policy is yet to be put in place, it is clearly the intention of the Government and its partners to continue with the promotion of ecotourism and the protection of the environment. There have, however, been some isolated attempts to move toward mass tourism for short-term economic gains without consideration to the negative impact on the country's fragile ecosystems.

Because of the experience of neighbouring countries, which have seen tourist numbers decline because of environmental problems, Belizeans are becoming more sensitive to the need to protect the environment. Tour operators and other stakeholders in the industry have a vested interest in maintaining the healthy state of the environment and are now becoming collaborators with environmental groups such as the Belize Audubon Society and other agencies who work to protect the environment.

| 6 |
Belize City, Belmopan and the district towns

The Anglican Cathedral of St John in Belize City (CUBOLA ARCHIVES)

Belize City is the undeniable heart of Belize from which all communications pulse outward. It is a port city founded on swamp, mangrove cayes and sand bars, and, according to legend, is built on a foundation of rum and gin bottles. Still today it sits barely above the high-water mark. It is often a dusty city and sometimes a muddy one, haphazard in some ways and yet captivating in its lack of sophistication. It is not a city that people are ambivalent about; nearly all – and not only visitors but also Belizeans – either hate it, or love it with a passion above simple loyalty. The City offers expensive hotels and modest guest houses, every conceivable type of restaurant, and discos that 'jam' to reggae and rock. Belize City is also a jumping-off place for the cayes and the Barrier Reef, for inland

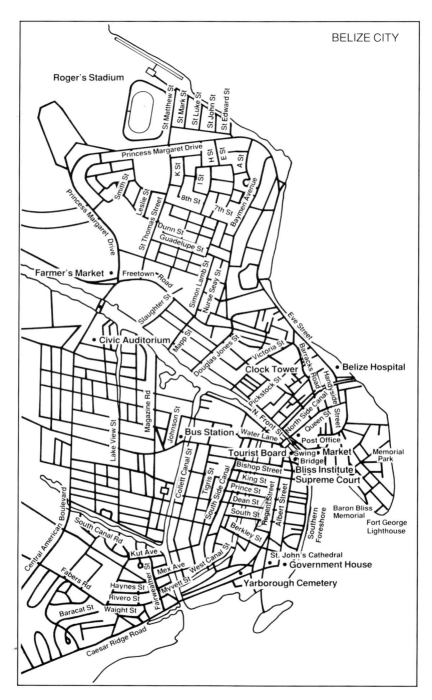

BELIZE CITY

Roger's Stadium

St Matthew St
St Mark St
St Luke St
St John St
St Edward St

Princess Margaret Drive

H St
E St
A St

K St
1 St

Baymen Avenue

Smith St
Leslie St
St Thomas Street

Princess Margaret Drive

8th St
7th St

Dunn St
Guadelupe St

Farmer's Market • Freetown Road

Simon Lamb St
Nurse Seay St

Slaughter St

Mapp St

Civic Auditorium

Douglas Jones St

Eve Street

Victoria St

Barracks Road

Clock Tower

Belize Hospital

Magazine Rd

Pickstock St

Handyside Street

Lake View St

Johnson St

N. Front St

North Side Canal

Queen St

Bus Station   Water Lane

Post Office

Tourist Board   Swing   Market
Bridge

Collett Canal St

Tigris St

Bishop Street

Bliss Institute

Memorial
Park

South Side Canal

King St

Supreme Court

Prince St

Regent Street

Albert Street

Central American Boulevard

South Canal Rd

Dean St
South St

Baron Bliss
Memorial

Berkley St

Southern
Foreshore

Fort George
Lighthouse

Kut Ave

Fabers Rd

Mex Ave

West Canal St

Fairweather St

Myvett St

St. John's Cathedral

Government House

Haynes St
Rivero St

Yarborough Cemetery

Baracat St   Waight St

Caesar Ridge Road

tours to Mayan ruins and rain forests, and to the Pine Ridge. A small municipal airport provides scheduled and charter flights by various carriers throughout the country; and the international airport links Belize with neighbouring Central American countries and the US.

Places worth a visit while in Belize City are the Anglican Cathedral (the oldest in Central America and a place where two Mosquito Coast Kings were crowned); Government House, the traditional home of the Governor General, and recently converted to a museum/cultural centre, is opposite the Cathedral; the Paslow Building on North Front Street, which houses the Post Office and the Magistrates' Courts; and the Bliss Institute which was endowed in 1926 by an Englishman with a Portuguese title, Baron Bliss, who left a fortune to the people of Belize in a perpetual trust fund to be used for cultural activities. He never set foot in Belize, but stayed aboard his yacht the *Sea King*, which lay offshore for a few months while he enjoyed the fishing in the Belizean waters before succumbing to a terminal illness.

There are a number of architecturally interesting private houses in the Fort George area, but hurricanes and a post-hurricane switch to concrete constructions have left ugly gaps in what once must have

The Roman Catholic Cathedral of the Holy Redeemer, Belize City (M J BOURNE)

Former Governor's residence, now Belize City House of Culture
(CUBOLA ARCHIVES)

been an area of traditional colonial buildings. The same is true elsewhere in the country, where there are remnants of public buildings and housing from colonial times. Belize City does not have the beautiful old plantation houses that are a prominent feature of some of the other Caribbean countries. Its slave quarters are restricted to a few low brick buildings to be seen at the back of some of the houses on Regent Street. Another interesting glimpse of history is the cholera cemetery on Caesar Ridge Road, which was built in the nineteenth century, above the ground in the manner of a Spanish cemetery. The Yarborough and Lords Ridge cemeteries are also worth a visit, as are the Technical College on Freetown Road with its long colonial veranda, and the old Belize City Hospital on Eve Street, which is similar in style, but badly in need of refurbishment.

With its 55,800 population, Belize City is fairly representative of Belize as a whole; it is over 69 per cent Creole, followed by Garifuna, East Indians, Mestizos, Maya and smaller groups of Lebanese, Chinese and Caucasian. From the rest of the country came traders in furniture, fruit and vegetables from among the Mennonite, Maya and Central American (Guatemalan, Salvadorean and Honduranean)

Haulover Creek and the Swing Bridge, Belize City
(CUBOLA ARCHIVES)

communities. Belize City is basically safe for tourists if care and sense are exercised. Tourists and visitors should check with their hotel or host when they arrive and ascertain which areas of the city to avoid. Just as in any other city, it is very foolish for strangers to wander around with cameras and gold chains around their necks in disreputable areas of the city. Petty crime, including bag-snatching and muggings, which did occur spasmodically in some areas in the city in the mid-1980s, has since been cracked down on severely by the authorities and has lessened considerably. As a rule, with persons who attempt to stop you in the street and 'hustle' boat trips, hotels and tours, it is best to thank them for the offer – and continue on your way.

The other districts provide few samples of outstanding architecture and what can be seen is often in need of a coat of paint. Only in the last decade has any attention at all been paid to preserving buildings of historical and architectural interest. An old and interesting iron-framed Belize City market, one of the few remaining examples of the type of market building once seen in dozens of Caribbean cities, was torn down in 1990 to make way for a modern building. At the time, the Government promised that this

41

The Court House in Belize City (M J BOURNE)

building would be rebuilt as an arts and crafts market in a new tourism development to be constructed on the north side of the city. A modern commercial center has replaced the old market in downtown Belize City; meanwhile a new tourism village on the north side of Belize City is being considered. The old fire station has been converted into a maritime museum and a more centrally located fire station was built in what is becoming a rapidly expanding port city, along with a new Customs House built in the Port Loyola area on the south side of the city. New landmarks also include a new multi-million dollar Central Bank building which was inspired by a Mayan motif. This new building was constructed on the site of the old Belize City Central Prison. This prison was also restored and will be used as a museum and national landmark.

A recent loan from the World Bank has allowed the Government of Belize to considerably improve the infrastructure of Belize City. With the rapid growth of auto traffic, a few traffic lights have been installed on the city's main streets. The old swing bridge which was built at the turn of the century, and which is one of three bridges connecting the north and south sides of the city, has recently received some major repairs and restoration.

Haulover Creek (opposite) (M J BOURNE)

43

The Swing Bridge in Belize City (RICHARD HUNT)

Belmopan

This artificially created capital of the nation has both the advantages and drawbacks of similar such cities. The city was built inland following the devastating Hurricane Hattie in 1961 which levelled out most of Belize City and other coastal towns. It is tidy, well planned but, according to many, also dull. That view is, however, often contradicted by those, mostly government employees, who live there. They point to the many community activities such as sports, concerts, art shows and the friendliness and intimacy of the town-dwellers, as proof that Belmopan is a 'caring and feeling' town where strangers are quickly made at home and where there is more communal participation than in most other towns in Belize. Belmopan has just 7,100 residents, but this population inflates overnight when a hurricane poses a threat to the country. A large

44

A timbermill at Belmopan (THE COMMONWEALTH INSTITUTE)

Vendors at Belmopan Market (CUBOLA ARCHIVES)

number of government officials visit it from their homes in Belize on a week-day basis, for this is where Parliament meets, and where most government offices are located. The people are friendly, despite the fact that they are continually being asked directions to Ministries and other addresses – the streets of Belmopan being curiously confusing to outsiders. Importantly, Belmopan is also the home of Belize's unique collection of Mayan artifacts and treasures. These are temporarily housed in the vaults of the Department of Archaeology.

There are fine hotels in Belmopan to suit all pockets and it is an excellent take-off point for various natural attractions including the Mountain Pine Ridge with the Rio On pools, the Thousand-Foot Falls, the Rio Frio Cave, Guanacaste Park and the Blue Hole.

Corozal

A charming, small town, of about 8,000 inhabitants, on the Bay of Chetumal just below the Mexican border, Corozal was almost totally wiped out by Hurricane Janet in 1955, although with little loss of life as the inhabitants were evacuated to the nearby Santa Rita hilltop, the site of an ancient Mayan city. Corozal was designed by the Belizean surveyor and town planner Henry Fairweather and rebuilt by British engineers after the hurricane, and so is the most planned

The **waterfront at Corozal Town** (CUBOLA ARCHIVES)

46

town in Belize apart from the new capital of Belmopan. It has wide, tree-lined streets, pleasant parks and a mixture of wood and cement housing. It was a rich little town prior to the partial collapse of the sugar cane industry in the early 1980s. It is only now recovering, as world sugar prices recover and the measures taken to diversify from cane into other agricultural products begin to take effect. Cerros, an exciting seaport of the ancient Maya, is a boat ride across the bay from Corozal. The attractive old market building, located on the foreshore, has recently been restored and is now the home of the Corozal Museum. However, this town is commercially virtually dead because of cheap Mexican goods which are available in the nearby Mexican City of Chetumal.

Orange Walk

This town is often called the 'Wild West' by imaginative US newspaper writers because of the district's connection with marijuana and cocaine smuggling. This 'trade', initially with home-grown marijuana and later extended by the 'trans-shipping' of cocaine from Colombia, began with the decline in sugar prices in the early 1980s and continues today despite extensive government efforts to crush it. Policing of the trade is made difficult by the wide,

Cane trucks at Tower Hill, Orange Walk (CUBOLA ARCHIVES)

mostly uninhabited areas in the north-west of the country and the ease with which small planes can enter and land undetected en route to the US with their lethal cargoes. Orange Walk Town itself, which now doubles Corozal in population, is a delightful inland oasis situated on the New River with good access to such archaeological sites as Lamanai and Cuello.

San Ignacio/Santa Elena

These twin towns of the west, separated by the Macal River but joined by the Hawkesworth suspension bridge, are today hilly, attractive reminders of the settling of Belize's exciting interior. San Ignacio is situated near the site of the ancient Mayan city of Cahal Pech, once an important trade and population centre that supervised the vast agricultural potential of the Belize River Valley. Recent excavations at Cahal Pech reveal two ball courts and the remains of the palaces of the Mayan aristocracy which dominated the lower strata of society inhabiting the valley below. Later, early colonial settlement came entirely by low draft river craft (pitpan) – until well into the twentieth century, and colonial trade was almost

Hawkesworth Bridge, San Ignacio (CUBOLA ARCHIVES)

exclusively confined to the lumber and logwood industry. Today both Santa Elena and San Ignacio are hubs of Belize's rapidly expanding ecotourism industry, acting as supply centers for the many small tourism lodges in the district.

Dangriga

This is one of the prettiest and least sophisticated of Belize's district towns. It is the heart of the country's multi-million-dollar citrus industry and rapidly growing as a tourism centre, both for its easy access to the many delightful offshore cayes and its proximity to the southern and largely unexplored areas of the Barrier Reef. Dangriga is also a major cultural and artistic centre, being home not only to some of Belize's finest painters (Pen Cayetano, Ben Nicholas) but also the place where the new Caribbean music craze, Punta Rock, originated and where Belize's best 'folk' bands are to be found. It has hotels to suit all pockets and easy, inexpensive bus services running north and south.

| 7 |
The six districts

A rally of the United Democratic Party at Placencia (LOU NICOLAIT)

A look at Belize from south to north will start with **Punta Gorda**, the most southern town, a charming little place on the seaside with a population of approximately 5,000 inhabitants and boasting wooden houses, two or three small hotels plus several guest houses. Punta Gorda is a true melting pot of Belize's many ethnic groups. A visit to the Fajina Craft Centre will introduce you to Mayan arts and crafts. A new tourist information centre is located on the sea front. For the more adventurous, an overnight stay in one of the village guest houses in the Mayan and Garifuna communities, a few miles from the town, is recommended.

Going north on the Southern Highway, the visitor will pass the recently restored Mayan centers of Lubaantun and Nim Li Punit. Further on you will find the banana plantations of **Big Creek**. Here, a shortage of labour has led to an upsurge of immigrants from Honduras, whose children will grow up as Belizeans.

The delightful fishing village of **Placencia** on the Placencia Peninsula can be reached by an all-weather road off the Southern Highway. This rapidly growing fishing village has retained its laid-back style and warm, friendly welcome for visitors while at the same time providing a variety of excellent accommodation for tourists. It is a perfect take-off point for fishing and snorkelling and provides a 'just lying in the sun' paradise reminiscent of story books.

Next comes the Stann Creek District and the rich orange belt of Belize. The principal town, with a population of nearly 8,000, is called **Dangriga**, meaning 'standing waters' in Garifuna. Dangriga is one of Belize's most delightful coastal towns, still untouched to a large extent by tourism or commercialism.

Inland is the lush Stann Creek Valley with its orange and grapefruit orchards. Here are signs of a vibrant industry growing by leaps and bounds. The two large processing factories lying on either side of the highway to Belmopan tell more than a story of healthy industry; they reflect a new trend in Belize – the buying out of traditional foreign interests by local entrepreneurs. Both processing

Dangriga Town (THE COMMONWEALTH INSTITUTE)

51

Cattle grazing in the fertile fields of the Cayo District (RICHARD HUNT)

houses went through this change in the late 1980s and early 1990s, and both have since upgraded their facilities to bring them on par with the best in the world. The citrus industry is in fact expanding so fast that it doubled its acreage in the 1980s and again in the 1990s.

The route then follows a completely paved Hummingbird Highway to the nation's capital, **Belmopan**. Belmopan is also the gateway to the west, to the Cayo District. This district is Belize's inland playground as it contains unique features offering unending adventure: the Pine Ridge with the famed Thousand-foot Falls, the double-ended Rio Frio Cave and the cascades of the Rio On; splendid cave systems – more than forty kilometres of connecting underground caverns and caves; ancient Mayan cities and temple sites (Caracol, Xunantunich, Cahal Pech, El Pilar); and, for the bird-watchers and the orchid-investigators, rivers for canoeing and forest wildlands for hiking or horseback-trekking. The twin towns of **Santa Elena** and **San Ignacio** (also simply called 'Cayo') have a combined population of 11,600. They are separated by one of Belize's highest and longest bridges, the Hawkesworth bridge, built by the British in 1945 and offering a picturesque view of the busy life going on in the Macal River below. As well as people boating, there may be children

52

swimming, women scrubbing clothes and men giving their cars or trucks a wash, an activity which is now prohibited under the environmental laws.

The scenic little town of San Jose Succotz still maintains many of the traditions of both Mayan and Mestizo cultures. There the ferry will take you across the Macal River to visit the ancient Mayan site of Xunantunich. A mile away the quiet border town of **Benque Viejo del Carmen**, with a population of 6,200, is the gateway to Guatemala.

Going north from Belize City, the Northern Highway reaches **Orange Walk Town** at Mile 53 and **Corozal Town** at Mile 96. Corozal, with a population of 8,100 (to Orange Walk's 16,600), shares with her northern sister town the now not so esteemed distinction of being a sugar town, built on the back of King Sugar in the good years and now rapidly trying to diversify. Its nearest sugar factory, which switched to ethanol production by the Petroleum Company of Jamaica, has temporarily closed down after Petrojam ceased operation. The present government, which was elected in the August of 1998, wants to re-open this factory as sugar prices once again begin to look favourable.

**The spectacular Privassion Cascade on
Mountain Pine Ridge (previous page)** (RICHARD HUNT)

Santa Elena is eight miles from Corozal, on the Mexican border. It will probably have the honour of becoming Belize's newest town as a commercial free-zone is being developed in that area.

San Pedro, the holiday resort town on Ambergris Caye, has a large population and recently achieved 'town' (as opposed to

Two views of San Pedro, Ambergris Caye
(CUBOLA ARCHIVES)

'village') status. With some 3,400 permanent residents, a local fishing industry and a unique tourism quality of its own, San Pedro is rapidly accumulating international acclaim. Someone not long ago called it the St Tropez of the Americas. Madonna popularised a song about the island called 'Isla Bonita'. Today every international flight into Belize brings its complement of visitors headed towards San Pedro with fishing rods and diving gear.

St George's Caye, Long Caye, Caye Chapel and Caye Caulker

These four cayes, all to the north of Belize City and all on the 'boat' route to San Pedro, are vastly different in nature.

St George's is one of Belize's original settlements and the site of the famous Battle of St George's Caye in 1798 in which Belize defeated a considerable Spanish armada. Today it is mostly home to private summer houses but has two resorts: St George's Lodge which is a dive resort and the Cottage Colony. The caye is an eight-mile skiff ride from Belize City.

Long Caye is a new development with a small hotel and good swimming and snorkelling. Many prominent Belizean families have bought house lots on the caye to build beach homes for themselves and their children. Long Caye is a twelve-mile skiff ride from Belize City.

Caye Chapel is a hotel island built initially by Pyramid Mining as a resort for their employees but long since opened as a public resort hotel. It caters for all manner of water sports and has a safe marina for power and sail boats.

Caye Caulker is the laid-back 'Ibiza' of Belizean cayes. Its small hotels and restaurants are excellent and yet inexpensive. This caye attracts more Europeans than any other resort area in Belize, has good snorkelling and diving on the nearby Barrier Reef, and a vibrant fishing industry ensuring a plentiful supply of seafood. It can be reached by skiff in forty-five minutes from

Two views of Caye Caulker (CUBOLA ARCHIVES)

Belize City. Skiffs to this and other cayes leave from the Marine Terminal on North Front Street. One of the best rides is with 'Chocolate', a veteran boatman with a skiff large enough to promise a comfortable ride.

A beach party at Goffs Caye (following page) (M J BOURNE)

Offshore Belize

There are several first class fishing lodges located offshore.

Turneffe Island Lodge   This famous lodge was built by Vic Barothy Senior at Caye Bokel in the late 1950s when he withdrew from his lodge on the Isle of Pines in Cuba after Castro's take-over and conversion of the island into the 'Isle of Youth'. It is one of Belize's finest and a great meeting place for local and international sports fishermen. Its gourmet restaurant is an attraction even for Belize City dwellers. A host of the famous – actors, writers, columnists – drop by during the season.

Turneffe Flats   This lodge lies on the north-east corner of the Turneffe atoll and is a favourite with fishermen from Texas and Colorado. It is simpler than Turneffe Lodge but offers excellent fishing and good food.

Blue Marlin Lodge   This excellent sporting lodge is located on South Water Caye offshore from Dangriga and has comfortable cabañas, a good restaurant and good snorkelling, diving and fishing.

Pelican Beach Resort Annex   Also on South Water Caye, the Pelican Beach Hotel (Dangriga) offers a cottage annex and large bunkhouse. This is an ideal and often used location for scientific, student and research groups and just a short boat ride away from the Smithsonian Research Station on Carrie Bow Caye.

Ricardo's Bluefield Range   This was originally a lobster camp and is comprised of cabins built on stilts over the shallow waters at Bluefield Range, just inside the Barrier Reef. It is inexpensive and provides exciting snorkelling, fishing and, in season, working the lobster pots with Ricardo.

Manta Reef Lodge   This pretty coconut island lodge, located at the southern tip of Glover's Reef, is a great favourite of scuba divers and fishermen and accesses some of the least explored and most exciting diving in all Belizean waters.

Glover's Reef Resort   This small resort achieved fame in the 1960s through a visit by the then Prime Minister of Canada, Pierre Trudeau.

It offers snorkelling, diving and, if desired, a quiet tropical island atmosphere to just lie around in.

Blackbird Caye Resort   This resort is located on the Turneffe Island atoll and features fifteen individual cabañas facing the sea, as well as an assortment of lounging and sporting activities. Groups and families with children are welcome here.

Hunting and Nicholas Cayes   These two most southern of Belize's cayes are popular resorts for visitors from Guatemala – including various past and serving presidents of Guatemala.

| 8 |
The Maya

Traditional Mayan dancers,
Southern Belize (CUBOLA ARCHIVES)

Mayan architects, sculptors, painters, weavers, potters and jewellery-makers produced at the height of their civilisation some of the finest works of art ever created. They erected cities covering as many as eighty square miles, linked and inter-linked by broad causeways. Placed around spacious plazas were huge temples and elegant palaces embellished with low-relief frescos, masks and stelae, and with multi-coloured narrative murals. Often these monumental works were inscribed with dates, for these master mathematicians had devised a calendar which told with precision the rhythms of the heavens. They also described in hieroglyph the important events in the lives of their dynastic rulers and the exploits of their mightiest warriors; in recent years, we have learned to decipher much of this particular form of writing.

Western frieze at Xunantunich Mayan site,
Cayo District (CUBOLA ARCHIVES)

The Maya also excelled in intensive farming techniques, using terracing, raised beds and sophisticated irrigation systems, all without the help of metal tools, the wheel, or beasts of burden.

· In launching the 'Ruta Maya' project in 1989, the then editor of *National Geographic Magazine*, Wilbur E. Garrett, wrote the following introduction:

The very word Maya evokes images of mystery-ancient pyramids soaring above trackless jungle, giant carved stones proclaiming artistic and intellectual prowess, a sudden and enigmatic demise.

Sometime before AD 250 – during the period known to archaeologists as the Preclassic – the first Mesoamerican culture that we can confidently call Maya borrowed ideas from neighbours, added its own ingredients, and created one of the most brilliant civilizations of antiquity amid the rain forest in the heart of the Yucatan Peninsula. In the ensuing Classic period, Mayan society endured for nearly six centuries as a dynamic population of nobles, priests, scribes, artists, craftsmen, warriors, and farmers located in cities ruled by a hereditary dynasty who claimed divine ancestry. The still unexplained

63

collapse of this world – perhaps hastened by agricultural failure due to climate change and the population pressure of as many as sixteen million people – was countered by the increasing strength of cultures to the west. The Postclassic period (circa AD 900 to AD 1,500) saw the rise of new centres of power, along with expanded trade routes and a new elite. Artifacts suggest a more cosmopolitan society but one still firmly grounded in traditional ways. The arrival of the Spaniards in the first decade of the sixteenth century violently closed this chapter of Mayan civilization.

Yet the Maya live today. At least four million descendants still speak the Maya languages. Though most are now Roman Catholic, they share the ancients' myths and practice rituals based on the ancestral view of the cosmos. Despite centuries of forced change, the Maya continue to leave an indelible mark on eastern Mesoamerica where the culture was born so long ago.

Today what remains of the Mayan treasures of those empiric days lies in museums, private collections, or still beneath the temples hidden deep in the jungle bush. In Belize, more than anywhere else in the Mayan world, most of the past is still buried. Great cities, similar to those which have been unearthed in Mexico, Guatemala and Honduras, lie dormant under blankets of earth, the roots of trees reaching down into their chambers; only recently has Belize's true importance in the ancient Mayan scheme of things started to be recognised.

Perfect examples of the neglect suffered by Belize's Mayan world are illustrated in the two Mayan cities of Caracol and Cahal Pech. The excavation, on a limited basis, of Caracol, now acknowledged as one of the great Mayan cities of over seventy square miles in area and with ten-mile-long causeways, was begun only a few years ago. It is principally a matter of money; tiny Belize, with a minute tax base, simply doesn't have the funds to reconstruct her amazing past. The same story is true of Cahal Pech. This small, three-acre citadel-like site sits literally on the outskirts of San Ignacio Town in Cayo District. Houses of the town sprawl to its very edge, no doubt built upon numerous ancient house mounds. Cahal Pech itself is a compact and amazingly well-preserved Mayan city centre which, at its height in the Classic period, was evidently the feudal heart of the immensely rich Upper Belize River Valley (in Mayan days the

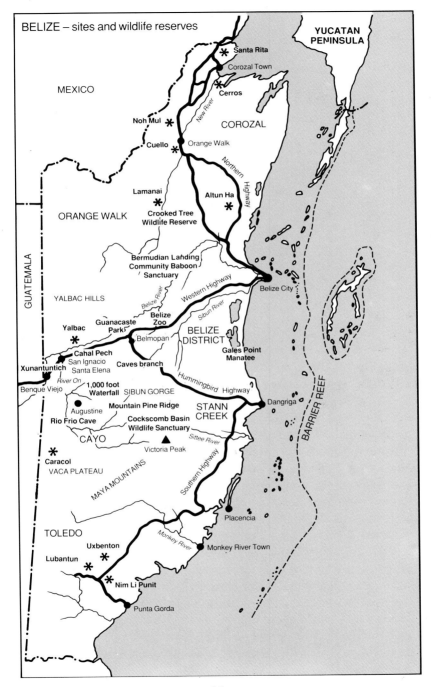

BELIZE – sites and wildlife reserves

YUCATAN PENINSULA

MEXICO

Santa Rita
Corozal Town
Cerros
Noh Mul
Cuello
Orange Walk
COROZAL

New River

Northern Highway

ORANGE WALK
Lamanai
Crooked Tree
Wildlife Reserve
Altun Ha

GUATEMALA

YALBAC HILLS

Bermudian Landing
Community Baboon
Sanctuary

Belize River
Western Highway
Belize City

Yalbac
Guanacaste
Park
Belize
Zoo
BELIZE
DISTRICT

Sibun River

Cahal Pech
San Ignacio
Santa Elena
Belmopan
Caves branch

Xunantuntich
Benque Viejo
River On

Gales Point
Manatee

1,000 foot
Waterfall
SIBUN GORGE
Hummingbird Highway

Augustine
Mountain Pine Ridge
Rio Frio Cave
Cockscomb Basin
Wildlife Sanctuary
STANN
CREEK

Dangriga

CAYO
Victoria Peak
Sittee River

BARRIER REEF

Caracol
VACA PLATEAU
Southern Highway

MAYA MOUNTAINS

Placencia

TOLEDO
Uxbenton
Lubantun
Monkey River
Monkey River Town

Nim Li Punit

Punta Gorda

Mayan ruins at Caracol (RICHARD HUNT)

breadbasket which must have fed an immense population). Cahal Pech surely was also an important trading centre, with river-borne goods such as cacao, ceramics, fruit, vegetables, meat and such luxury items as jade and obsidian arriving from Caribbean seaside ports and possibly from as far away as the Pacific.

Today, looking down from the heights of Cahal Pech, it is not hard to imagine the sprawling, thatched-roofed township below, spreading down to the river's edge and expanding probably to the junction of the Macal and Mopan rivers some three miles away. The view would have also taken in the distant Mayan cities of Xunantunich and El Pilar, other guardian towns of the same rich agricultural valley. It is surmised that Xunantunich eventually superseded Cahal Pech in importance.

Although a thousand years ago the Maya used sophisticated agricultural methods such as raised-beds and complex irrigation systems, today many Mayan farmers use the archaic method of slash-and-burn agriculture to make their *milpas*. In olden days, a stick with a hardened sharp point was dug into the ground to make room for three to five corn seeds per hole. A similar planting stick, although sometimes metal-tipped, is still used in the same manner today.

A corner of the Mayan ruins at Cahal Pech, San Ignacio (RICHARD HUNT)

Little of the ancient tradition of weaving and exquisite embroidery which still survives today in Mesoamerica is to be seen in Belize. Other art forms are only now being introduced as seen, for example, in the slate and stone carvings done by the Garcia sisters, the hand-made pottery decorated with traditional Mayan motifs of David Magaña of Succotz, and the fine baskets and embroideries from the villages in Toledo.

Town market days are, in Belize as in other societies, a good place to see the perpetuation of traditional lifestyles. The Saturday market in Punta Gorda is one of the most colourful in the country. Here, Mayan Indians come from their villages, sometimes long distances, bringing produce and other goods to sell or to trade. They assemble in the heart of town on the sea front, from early dawn onwards – market day as it has always been and, hopefully, as it will continue to be.

Mayan Kekchi Strings from San Pedro Colombia,
Toledo District (CUBOLA ARCHIVES)

Altun Ha, the Mayan ruins
(CUBOLA ARCHIVES)

The Temple of the Jaguar, Lamanai (RICHARD HUNT)

Belize is proud of the most famous Mayan doctor-priest in Central America, Don Eligio Panti, who lived in the western village of San Antonio. He practised the ancient art of spiritual and physical healing in his thatch-roofed clinic in the hills of Cayo until he died there at the age of 101 in 1997. Furthermore, through the dedication of his student, Dr Rosita Arvigo, his knowledge of herbal medicines will not be lost. The National Cancer Institute of Washington, DC, is now studying Belizean plants for possible medicinal usage.

Belize's Mayan past and descriptions of many of her Mayan cities can be better appreciated by reading *Warlords and Maize Men*, published by Cubola Productions and available at book shops in Belize. It lists fifteen major sites and includes many site plans and photographs.

The best advice for travellers seeking information about Mayan ruins and/or travel operators is to consult the Belize Tourism Industry Association on Park Street, or the Belize Tourist Board on North Front Street, on arrival in Belize. It would take an entire book to list Mayan ruins and appropriate tour agents. Most hotels also have connections with tour guides and companies.

| 9 |
Wildlife

(Contributed by Sharon Matola, director and founder of the Belize Zoo)

While no species of wildlife is endemic to Belize, this little tropical nation harbours a plethora of wild animals, some considered endangered species throughout their geographical range, and some standing on the brink of extinction in other parts of the region. Due to widespread deforestation, wildlife throughout Central America has steadily decreased during the past twenty-five years. Most of Belize, however, remains forested and undeveloped, and this has led to a situation where the natural heritage of Belize, its birds, mammals and reptiles, live in relatively healthy populations.

Belize may be small in area, but within its 8,867 square miles lie distinct and varied habitats. The savannahs and lowlands are a refuge for rare water fowl such as the wood stork, the jabiru stork, and the roseate spoonbill. The riverine forests provide habitats for pumas, tapir and eagles. The mountainous regions of the country ensure a niche for the jaguar, the brocket deer, and the secretive margay cat.

A steady growth of environmental awareness in Belize over the past few years has resulted in a national sense of pride – the people of a country expressing a protective spirit for their unique natural resources.

The Government of Belize has designated large parks and reserves throughout the country for the preservation of wildlife. Thirty miles north of Belize City lies the Crooked Tree Wildlife Sanctuary. Besides providing a home for numerous mammals, such as the anteater and the coatimundi, the most dramatic species that lives and breeds at Crooked Tree Lagoon is the magnificent jabiru stork, *Jabiru mycteria*. This stork, the largest bird in all the Americas, stands four feet high and has a wingspan between eight

Jabiru chicks (opposite) (RICHARD HUNT)

and ten feet. Belize has the largest breeding colony of jabiru storks in all of Central America. They are most often seen at Crooked Tree Lagoon between the months of November and May. At the height of the breeding season, the neckband of this bird is brilliant red in colour. Both parent storks care for the young, usually three in number, until they have fledged. In Belize, aerial surveys, conducted on an annual basis by the Belize Audubon Society, carefully monitor the nesting activity of jabiru storks.

Located south-west of Crooked Tree Lagoon is the Community Baboon Sanctuary at Bermudian Landing. The village of Bermudian Landing lies along the Belize River and was once an important site during the days of logwood and mahogany timbering. Today, the village of Bermudian Landing is becoming well known for its population of some 800 black howler monkeys, *Aloutta pigra*, which live there. The largest of the two species of monkeys in Belize, the black howler monkey, or 'baboon' as it is locally known, spends a good deal of time eating, sleeping and howling in the giant fig trees that line the riverbank. They eat the young leaves and the ripe fruits of the fig tree, and the roar of the male howler announcing his territory can be heard for miles. This howl, often described as a

An adult black howler monkey (RICHARD HUNT)

'roar', is one of the loudest calls produced by any animal. Although both sexes vocalise, the ferocious-sounding howling that characterises this species is rendered by the male howler monkey. The howl is produced by air passing through the cavity within an enlarged bone in the throat, the hyoid. It is much larger in the male howler monkey than in the female.

The people living in Bermudian Landing have joined together and agreed not to remove the trees along the riverside so that their monkeys will always have a home in their village. While howler monkeys live from southern Mexico down into the forest of South America, the species that occurs in Belize is remarkably rare. *Aloutta pigra* inhabits only pockets of forest in southern Mexico, Guatemala and Belize. There are other animals to be found within this riverine forest. The jaguarundi, *Felix jaguarundi*, the smallest of the wild cats in Belize, the little red brocket deer, *Amazona americana*, and the gregarious collared peccary, *Dicotyles tajacu*, also live in the Bermudian Landing Community Baboon Sanctuary.

Belize still maintains a healthy population of jaguars, and government efforts to protect them have led to the formation of laws that forbid their hunting. Belize also has the world's only jaguar preserve, the Cockscomb Basin Jaguar Preserve, in the Stann Creek District. This preserve, created in 1986 and then enlarged from 3,000 acres to 102,000 acres in 1990, attracts thousands of visitors annually.

The jaguar, *Panthera onca*, a stunning member of the cat family and the largest cat in the Americas, was once found from the southwestern United States, down through Mexico and Central America, and throughout South America. Today its range has been severely reduced, and this beautiful cat is considered an endangered species.

Although the jaguar is classified as one of the big cats, it does not roar, a characteristic that is shared by the other members of the genus *Panthera*. The preferred habitat of the jaguar is dense forests or swamps. They are rarely found in areas without good cover and seem to favour easy access to water. Jaguars climb trees, but they hunt on the ground. Food for a jaguar in Belize would include armadillo, deer, peccary, birds and rodents. Jaguars are also known to fish and they excel at swimming. Solitary in their habits, the jaguar is believed only to keep company with others of its species during the breeding season. After a gestation period of 120 days, the female will give birth to a litter consisting of two or four young. The cubs are blind at birth but open their eyes after a week. Staying with their mothers for two years, the cubs learn the ways of life in the forest. At the age of three, the jaguar is sexually mature.

The four other species of cats that live in Belize are also found within the sanctuary. *Felis wedii*, the small and graceful margay cat, rare throughout Central America, lives high in the tree tops and is nocturnal by nature. Small birds and rodents are what these cats subsist on, and their arboreal habitats also determine their breeding habits. The margay cat nests and raises its young in the forest canopy, not on the ground. *Felis pardalis*, the ocelot, another spotted cat, is bigger than its cousin, the margay. The ocelot is more active in the day than at night and therefore is able to compete within the same niche as the smaller margay. At one time, not all that long ago, the ocelot was in great demand by the fur industry, and was the most frequently hunted small cat in Latin America. In 1975, Britain alone imported 76,838 ocelot skins. Today, the ocelot is endangered throughout its geographical range. In Belize, to hunt an ocelot is in direct violation of the country's wildlife laws.

Very little is known about the jaguarundi, *Felix jaguarundi*. This small cat feeds on birds and rodents but, due to its reticent nature, the jaguarundi is not often seen. There are two colour phases of this cat, one being grey-black, and the other reddish-brown, the colour phase which occurs more often in Belize.

The puma, *Felis concolour*, also shares the Cockscomb Basin Jaguar Preserve with its feline relatives. Known in Belize as the 'red tiger', the puma coexists and competes in the same area as the jaguar, but the two species share territory without conflict. Studies in the Cockscomb Basin Jaguar Preserve have shown the re-occurrence of jaguar and puma tracks in similar regions, indicating that the two different species overlap in their territorial range.

One of the rarest parrots in all of Central America is found in the sanctuary, the scarlet macaw, *Ara macao*. It is believed that less than fifty pairs still live in Belize, and it is hoped that, since they are now protected in the country, their numbers will gradually begin to increase. Scarlet macaws live in pairs and their loud calls are heard mostly at dawn and during the late afternoon hours.

Another rare bird of the reserve is the stately and magnificent king vulture, *Sarcorhamphus papa*. It is the largest of the New World

An ocelot (opposite) (RICHARD HUNT)

74

vultures found in Central America, and soars high above the Belizean landscape, keeping a careful watch out for its smaller cousins, the turkey vulture, *Cathartes aura*, and the black vulture, *Caragyps atrutus*. When the king vulture spots a group of these vultures feeding, it will swoop down and, in behaviour which can be described accurately as intimidating, will rid the carcass of the smaller scavengers, thus making their meal its very own. King vultures are born completely black in colour and, over a period of eight years, their dark plumage gradually changes until the bird is predominantly white with a brightly-coloured head. A mature king vulture has a wing span of up to seven feet.

The Central American tapir, *Tapirus bairdii*, another species considered to be endangered, lives and breeds in the Cockscomb Basin. These primitive ungulates are related to the horse and the rhinoceros and have been roaming this part of the earth since the days of the dinosaurs. They are gentle herbivores, and are chiefly nocturnal in their habits. As with other species of tropical animals, massive destruction of their forest habitats during the past twenty-six years has forced them to the very brink of extinction, but in the reserves of Belize they are guaranteed a home in which they can increase their numbers. With great pride, Belize has rightly designated the tapir as its national animal.

The National bird of Belize is the keel-billed toucan, *Ramphastos sulfuratus*. It has a huge, colourful bill which appears heavy and cumbersome but, being hollow and grooved inside, does not hamper this bird from flying high above the sanctuary's rivers and streams. Keel-billed toucans are usually seen in flocks of eight or more and, although their forest diet consists chiefly of fruits and nuts, they are known to rob the nests of other birds and eat the young.

Some of these species – and many more – inhabit other reserves in Belize as well, and much of the uncultivated or undeveloped land of the country serves as unofficial sanctuary. It goes without saying that together these areas harbour untold varieties of plant life, including the exotic-wood trees on which the colonial economy was based – logwood, mahogany, cedar, rosewood and fiddlewood – as well as other tropical trees such as the gumbolimbo, the sapodilla (chicle) tree, and numerous *Palmae* including the coconut, the cohune and the royal palm. Mangroves along the coast and in the lagoons create a whole network of habitats for a myriad of water-loving birds and creatures. Many trees host orchids and bromeliads

An adult brown pelican at Caye Caulker (RICHARD HUNT)

in great variation. A variety of plant species play an important part in 'traditional medicine': roots, bark and leaves which have been chopped and dried are used in infusions as teas or baths, folk remedies widely used throughout the country to this day. Because of the pristine condition of much of Belize's forests, and of accessibility to the knowledge of Belizean healers, New York Botanical Gardens and the Cancer Research Institute of Washington DC are gathering material and data from Belize to use in their research into herbal medicines.

The uniqueness of the country's fauna and flora is imparted to the people of Belize through progressive wildlife education programmes that are regularly sponsored by the Belize Audubon Society and the Belize Zoo. The Belize Zoo also maintains a collection of Belizean mammals, birds and reptiles, and has an active school programme that sees children from every district in the country pass through its

Black orchid (Kevin Schafer/NHPA)

gates each month. It is the steady, growing pride in the wildlife of Belize by the people of the nation which will ensure the preservation of this irreplaceable natural heritage for generations to come.

An important recent addition to Belize's parks and reserves is the 90,000-acre Bladen Reserve in the Toledo District. This is a unique high mountain valley area with many rare species of plant life and the undisturbed home of many species of wildlife. It was declared a national park by the former Deputy Prime Minister and Minister of Natural Resources, Florencio Marin, in 1990.

Local and up-to-date information on the Belize Zoo and Tropical Education Centre at mile 30 on the Western Highway, on the many parks and reserves of Belize, and on the ongoing courses about archaeology, wildlife and natural history are best obtained from the BTIA, the Tourist Board or hotels, upon arrival in Belize. Information is also available directly from the Zoo or from the Belize Audubon Society on Fort Street.

Note: *Jungle Walk*, by Katie Stevens, is an informative and entertaining field guide to the birds and beasts of Belize. *The Environment of Belize: our life support system* provides the visitor with an excellent introduction to ecology, ecosystems and conservation efforts of Belize.

| 10 |
Belize's wondrous underwater world

Belize's reef is a fabled fairyland. Words cannot adequately describe the wondrous, ever-changing world of underwater Belize, the languorous, sometimes breathless silence and the extraordinarily colourful nature of its inhabitants: the living corals, the crabs, shrimp and lobster, the conch in its elegant shell, and fishes in unending shapes and sizes.

In his book, *Coral Kingdoms*, Carl Rossler says of his visit to Belize:

One of the largely unspoiled wonders of the Caribbean is Lighthouse Reef, some sixty miles out to sea from the coast of Belize. My visits to these exquisitely rich gardens of coral and fish are always tinged with sadness, because I realise that riches like those of Belize were once everywhere in the Caribbean. This realisation is not merely my own personal reaction; it is a distillation of stories heard from hundreds of old-time fishermen and spearmen. There are men in their forties and fifties today who, as teenagers, speared off the upper Florida Keys when they were rich and clear; men in their thirties who knew Curaçao, Cozumel, Cayman and other islands when they swarmed with big reef predators such as grouper and snapper. Today at Lighthouse Reef one feels transported back in time, for on these reefs the big groupers still roam.

Lighthouse Reef is now a protected national park and, luckily for Belize, an enlightened government is taking further measures to preserve Belize's reef against the ills that have destroyed reef systems in other parts of the world. Hol Chan, at the south end of Ambergris Caye, is Belize's first marine reserve. It was declared a national preserve in 1987 when tourism, in its appetite for fish and lobster, was already making heavy inroads into the island's seafood supply. In its first twelve months, the reserve was able to show local

Lighthouse Reef from the air (RICHARD HUNT)

fishermen that, far from depleting their catch as they had feared, the establishment of Hol Chan had resulted in better fishing in their waters than had existed before. It is just the first of several such reserves planned for the reef as a whole, including restrictive legislation that is in the pipeline for the famous southern atoll at Glover's Reef.

The beauty of Belize's Barrier Reef (which was declared a World Heritage Site by UNESCO in 1997), is enhanced by the fact that much of it is easily accessible and yet it takes considerable effort to get to the rest. This puts it in reach of locally run and locally based tourism establishments while, at the same time, assuring that far-off areas of the reef will remain pristine long into the future of their industry – in a state of natural good health. As a result, even the youngest Belizean dive guide starting out in the business will advise visitors to the reef about how they can help to keep it that way –

Fish swim amongst the different kinds of coral on the Barrier Reef (RICHARD HUNT)

beginning with the warning that even accidentally touching coral, with hand or flipper, may cause it to die. Already spearfishing with air tanks is outlawed for tourists and those in the dive trade are today converting their clients into 'lookers' rather than hunters, the underwater camera usurping the spear. A relatively new money-earner for Belize, reef diving is growing quickly. It is also watching its own expansion cautiously in acknowledgement that too fast may mean too much, and too much may convert success today into failure tomorrow.

No mention of Belize's reef would be complete without reference to the famous Blue Hole, north of Lighthouse Reef, which Jacques Cousteau investigated in the 1970s. Located some forty miles offshore, it is still today a unique diving experience, a mysterious underwater world hundreds of feet deep which relatively few divers have explored and from which all emerge with a renewed respect for nature's marvellous diversity. Just snorkelling in the Blue Hole, above the seemingly bottomless indigo underwater pit, creates an overwhelming feeling of being on the edge of space.

The reef has something to offer everyone, from small children bobbing about in life jackets, to snorkellers drifting over the amazing fish flitting among the corals of the shallows, to professionals and diving *aficionados* who want the best, the most spectacular and sometimes the dangerous. For this latter group there are under-island caves, tunnels and deep sink holes opening into vast underwater caverns which can only be safely explored by using rope guidelines. There are safety restrictions on some of these caves, and others which to date have kept their secrets to themselves.

A dozen books cannot tell the full story of the reef and its creatures. Photographs help, but true knowledge of the reef comes from the experience itself and it is never too late for that; a seventy-four-year-old woman was among novice divers at one Belizean dive resort recently, learning all the techniques of day and night wall diving!

If you think the reef is beautiful by day, at night the corals come to life to reveal a veritable wonderland, and exquisite infinity of colour and design.

**The famous Blue Hole
north of Lighthouse Reef** (RICHARD HUNT)

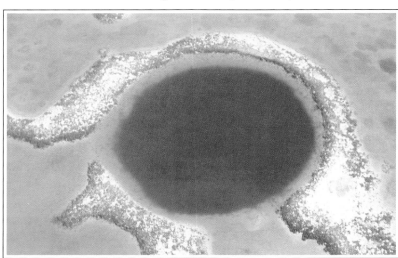

| 11 |
A guide to hotels, restaurants and shopping

The Radisson Fort George Hotel, Belize City (M J BOURNE)

Belize is a paradise for those travellers who appreciate the simple, the friendly and the real. It is not a playground for the very rich and spoiled, it is not a place for those who are looking for the bright lights of Las Vegas or St Tropez, and it is not any sort of replica of any other tourism destination anywhere in the world. It is a country of startling contrast, of unsurpassed natural beauty and offers on-the-ground and under-sea adventures – exploring caves, jungles, rivers, uninhabited tropical islands and the magnificent Barrier Reef.

Food in restaurants, hotels and guest houses is, from end to end of the country, simple but good. The staple diet of most Belizeans is rice and beans with either chicken, fish or beef. This is also a very popular dish with tourists and very different from the rice and beans in other parts of the Caribbean. The difference stems from the fact that in Belize coconut milk (i.e. milk extracted from grated coconut) is usually used to cook the rice, giving it an attractive, slightly nutty flavour. Another especially Belizean meal is 'boil-up', which consists of a wide variety of root vegetables, including cassava and yams, cooked with pig tail and fish. An exciting fact about food in Belize is the easy and extremely reasonably priced availability of choice fresh fish, lobster, shrimp and also, over the last ten years, good beef. Lobster and fish, which are price controlled on the local market, are available at approximately BZ$12 per lb and excellent fillet of beef sells for about the same. This tasty and wholesome diet accounts for the general good health of Belize's population.

Tap water is drinkable in all the districts although in some of the island communities, including San Pedro, visitors are advised to stick to bottled – or rain-water. Accommodation ranges from first class to simple in the extreme, and the prices reflect the range. For example, there are Belize City and San Pedro hotels which charge up to US$120 per night but a stone's throw away will be small hotels and guest houses charging less than US$10 per night. The Belize Tourist Board, on North Front Street in Belize City, provides a free list of all hotels and guest houses throughout the country and the charges.

Souvenir shopping ranges from all manner of wood carvings to basket ware, coral jewellery, paintings and Mayan weavings and stone carvings. Most items are locally produced but some come from Mexico, Guatemala and El Salvador. Reproductions of clay and jade artifacts are also available. Tourists are advised to ask sellers for written proof that the goods are 'copies'; otherwise vigilant immigration and customs officers in both Belize and the US may detain travellers if they are suspected of smuggling real artifacts out of the country.

There follows a brief guide to hotels and restaurants in Belize City and lodges throughout the country. The Tourist Board has a full list for visitors.

Hotels – Belize City and environs

There are a number of good large hotels in Belize City and also many smaller hotels, pensions and guest houses. Here is a quick rating in alphabetical order.

Top hotels

Bellevue Hotel (Southern Foreshore)
Belize Biltmore Plaza (at about mile 3 Northern Highway)
Radisson Fort George (Fort George area)
Fiesta Inn, formerly Ramada Royal Reef (Barracks waterfront)
The Great House (Fort George area)

Less expensive hotels

Chateau Caribbean
El Centro
Hotel Mopan

Guest houses

Colton House
Fort Street Restaurant and Guest House
Glenthorne Manor
North Front Street Guest House
Seaside Guest House
Isabel Guest House

Restaurants

An award for excellent food and an unequalled view over Belize City
and the Fort area waterfront must be given to the new rooftop
restaurant and bar at the recently redesigned Villa Hotel. All the top
hotels and the Chateau Caribbean and El Centro have good public
restaurants. The Fort George has a restaurant overlooking the sea
and also serves food in its first floor air-conditioned bar; the Chateau
specialises in seafood; and El Centro is noted for its Belizean food.

Fine dining in a romantic atmosphere can be had at Fort Street
Restaurant in the Fort George area, and at Mango's in the Barracks.
The Smoking Mermaid at the Great House features a tropical garden
restaurant. The Fiesta Inn has two restaurants including the open air
Calypso. The Bellevue Hotel on the south side has its spacious
indoor restaurant and has also just opened an attractive garden bar
and restaurant. For sheer value, Macy's on Bishop Street on the
south side of the city is hard to beat. It specialises in Belizean food
– including game meats. It was a favourite haunt of Harrison Ford
when he was in Belize making 'Mosquito Coast'.

The Radisson Fort George Marina (N GILLARD)

Besides these choices there are dozens of small, good, inexpensive restaurants scattered around the city. Good Mexican food is served very cheaply at 'Mexican Corner' on King Street, and Chinese food is served at a number of restaurants throughout the city.

Shopping

The small but thriving handicraft industry offers the visitor a variety of handicrafts made out of local woods such as sericote and rosewood, larger items made out of mahogany, and hand carved and hand painted furniture. Belize's newest 'mall', located on the ground floor of the Greathouse, has a bookstore, wine and cigar store, a boutique and an art gallery.

Cubola Productions publishes a variety of well researched and attractively presented books which can be found in most giftshops. Stonetree Records CD's and cassettes provide a taste of Belize's rich musical cultural heritage. Also check out The Image Factory, a non-profit organization that promotes and represents local artists through their gallery and art shop on North Front Street. Belize's weekly newspapers give visitors an inside glimpse of local happenings.

86

Belize City's main supermarkets are Brodie's (also a department store), RoMac's and Save U. There are numerous small shops and boutiques throughout the city, and souvenirs and handicrafts can be purchased from street vendors or from the hotel gift shops, as well as a wide range of books and T-shirts. For the unique in T-shirts and for other suitable gifts, Isabel's 'Go-Tees' on Regent Street is well worth a visit. Baskets and some other handicrafts can also be purchased from the Belize Chamber of Commerce and Industry National Crafts Centre in the Fort George area of Belize City. These items can be shipped to the visitor. You can also shop at the maritime terminal, the airport's duty free shop, and at the giftshops which most hotels have.

Belize's jungle lodges

Throughout Belize, and especially in the north and west, there are a number of jungle lodges which give a unique flavour to travel in Belize. They are comfortable, usually provide a wide range of activities such as horse-back riding, caving and jungle tours, and are highly individualistic in character.

In the north:

Chan Chich Lodge at Gallon Jug, Orange Walk District. This lodge must truly be seen to be believed. It is the ultimate in jungle comfort, a work of art created in the very heart of a Mayan ruin. Located in the middle north-west of what used to be the old Belize Estates timber land, Chan Chich was built by Tom and Josie Harding from Colorado for Belizean businessman Barry Bowen. Wood cut from the property was used to construct the lodge and cabañas, situated so that no permanent damage would result to the surrounding Mayan ruin. This ruin, and its many pyramids, rises majestically on all sides of the lodge but does not overpower the surroundings. They feel a natural part of the whole, and the lodge and cabañas blend in as if welcomed by the original builders and inhabitants.

Just getting to Chan Chich can be both an adventure and full of surprises, either coming in by air to Gallon Jug, or driving by way of Orange Walk and Blue Creek. The air trip takes just half an hour from Belize City and usually the pilot will fly over Lamanai if asked, providing passengers with a fine view of this remote lagoon-fronted Mayan city. By car, and something sturdy is recommended, the route via the Mennonite settlement at Blue Creek passes Belize's only hydroelectric plant (built by the Mennonites to power Blue Creek village), an old Super Constellation aeroplane high on a hill (from which the Mennonites salvaged most of the wiring to build their electric plant), and Programme for Belize land where archaeologists and naturalists are currently classifying flora, fauna and the spectacular La Milpa archaeological site. This can be visited by arrangement with the Programme for Belize office in Belize City. Further Mennonite influence can be seen after passing Barry Bowen's hilltop home farm at Gallon Jug and approaching Chan Chich. This is the suspension bridge linking up to the lodge and spans what in the dry season looks more like a drain than a river; but in the wet it becomes a raging torrent more than thirty feet wide and running ten feet deep.

At the lodge itself there is a wide choice of activities which include some of the best bird watching in the country, superb walks and trails, interesting visitors and relaxation. The walks nearby the lodge are exciting and yet easy, even for the elderly or very young, and are unforgettable in their extraordinary mixture of high rain forest and the multiple bird life in the canopy above.

The reputation of the lodge's dining room, and its convivial bar, are a drawcard in themselves and the food and good wine list brings in the scientists and researchers working nearby at Programme for Belize land, and friends and visitors. Some, occasionally and most arduously, come on the 'never to be ventured' back-track from San Ignacio! This is not advised – ever!

Stepping into the cabañas at Chan Chich is like stepping from the jungle into simple but comfortable luxury. Polished and oiled woodwork, all painstakingly finished, offer a reminder that Belize furniture was once highly prized in Europe; and quiet but colourful drapes and furnishings speak of the great care and attention that has been put into making the lodge what it is.

It is advisable **always** to telephone in advance for lodging or meals because of the long distance to return if the lodge is full.

The Thousand-foot Falls in Mountain Pine Ridge
(opposite) (THE COMMONWEALTH INSTITUTE)

Lamanai Outpost Lodge is an excellent lodge located in the remote area of Orange Walk District. It offers 18 rooms with private baths (hot and cold water), fans and 24-hours-a-day power. These thatch-roofed cabañas are made out of natural timber. Here you can enjoy the view of the lagoon, Lamanai Mayan ruins, and gardens. There is also a spotlight night river safari, and canoeing, swimming and birding can be enjoyed. This is a magnificent place to do archeological or other educational/research programs. It has a meeting facility for 32.

Maruba is located on the old Belize City Road near Maskall. This attractive lodge is situated in hundreds of acres of high bush and jungle country some 35 miles north of Belize City and boasts of being 'an oasis of Charm and Grace' – as indeed it is. It is just a few miles from the ancient Mayan city of Altun Ha where the famous 'jade head' was found – the largest jade carving ever found in the Americas. It has not only a delightful swimming pool laid out in an attractive garden setting but also an open-air Japanese tub and professional massage. An imaginatively conceived open-air, plant-surrounded restaurant offers excellent food.

A Belizean timber yard (THE COMMONWEALTH INSTITUTE)

90

The lodge was built by the Nicholson family, and they themselves are an exotic mixture of Belizean, US and European backgrounds with a European/US upbringing. The lodge offers cabaña accommodation, tours to Lamanai and Altun Ha, walks in the rain forest and even a one-day adventure escape that includes accommodation, a hike, massage, mineral bath and meals. A further bonus is that Maruba can also be reached by an interesting skiff ride from San Pedro, Ambergris Caye. Alternatively, visitors to Maruba can take a day or two and journey by water to San Pedro. Alexandra and her husband Mike, her sister Sissie, and brother, Nicky, are the family workhorses with Dr and Mrs Nicholson very much behind them in their efforts. The lodge provides a perfect venue for a relaxing day away from the city or a delightful get-away hideout for a longer stay.

In the west:
Chaa Creek Cottages is Belize's most famous jungle lodge. It is located west of San Ignacio Town towards the Guatemalan border about three miles off the main road. It is owned by Mick and Lucy Fleming who built the lodge in 1979 from a small, run-down and abandoned farm on Chaa Creek. They constructed one small

Ecotourists relaxing at Chaa Creek resort, Cayo District
(CUBOLA ARCHIVES)

thatched-roofed tourist cabin at first, more for friends to stay in than with any idea of starting a major business, but as more and more guests turned up, Mick and Lucy expanded to meet the demand. Today Chaa Creek Cottages has 19 thatched-roofed cabañas delightfully sited in a landscaped garden. Whereas, in the early days, guests had to take pot luck at Lucy's kitchen table, today there is a fully staffed gourmet restaurant and garden bar. Chaa Creek offers guests jungle and Mayan site tours, horseback riding, hiking expeditions into mostly unexplored areas of the Vaca Plateau, cave trips and canoeing on the Macal River. Don't miss the Natural History Center and the Butterfly Breeding Station.

Just next door to Chaa Creek is the Panti Medicinal Trail where visitors can take a tour of some of the useful plants used in bush medicine. It is located on Ix Chel Farm where Dr Rosita Arvigo and her husband, Dr Greg Shropshire, prepare plants, roots and herbs for shipment for medical research in the US. At their gift shop, herbal remedies and cosmetics made on the premises are available.

DuPlooys is a relatively new lodge started in the mid 1980s by Ken and Judy DuPlooy, also on the site of a farm but a little higher up the Macal River from Chaa Creek. It is a charming hilltop garden lodge with excellent swimming in the Macal River. Ken is an avid gardener and has collected and nurtured many different varieties of jungle vines, flowers and orchids which are now attracting the attention of horticulturalists from many parts of the world as word of his collection, 'Belize Botanic Gardens', spreads.

Maya Mountain Lodge is on the road to the Mountain Pine Ridge from San Ignacio Town. The lodge specialises in educational and scientific groups but also has individual cabañas nestled among landscaped gardens. It was started in the mid 1980s by Bart and Susie Mickler and has since become a popular resort.

Windy Hill Resort is on the western outskirts of San Ignacio and has fine views from its hilltop cabañas. A must for guests is the excellent riding stable, from which both unescorted and guided riding trips along the Mopan River valley are popular.

Parrot Nest is a small eco-lodge 3 miles from San Ignacio just outside the village of Bullet Tree. It lies on the Mopan River and has three houses and cabins and good home-cooked food. It is well recommended, and best contacted through Eva's Restaurant.

Casa Maya EcoResort is a new lodge at about mile 68 on the Western Highway. It offers a range of accommodation: luxury cabins, guesthouses for budget travellers, and a $5-a-night campground.

Caesar's Place, which has one of Belize's best giftshops, is located at mile 60 on the Western Highway. It has four rooms and a campground with hoop-ups and security. There is also a restaurant and bar, and live music on some nights.

Black Rock is owned by Caesar's and is a riverside lodge located on the Macal River. It is off the beaten track – use the same turnoff from the Western Highway as Chaa Creek and DuPlooys, and from there follow the signs. This lodge provides a jungle adventure.

Tree Stop is a small, budget lodge outside the village of Succotz near the point where the ferry crosses to Xunantunich. It has an excellent live butterfly house plus museum, also nature trails and a restaurant. Other butterfly houses can be found at Chaa Creek Lodge and at Greenhills Botanical Collection at mile 8 on the Pine Ridge Road.

Mountain Equestrian Trails (MET) started out purely as a riding establishment but now has delightful cabañas and a good restaurant that is open to the public. It is located on the road into the Pine Ridge from Georgeville. MET's horseback expeditions, with alternative routes into the Pine Ridge, the Maya Mountains, the Chiquibul forest and even to Caracol, are famous throughout the adventure tourism world. Their horses are suitable for all classes of rider, from beginners to experts.

Pine Ridge Lodge is a new small lodge in the heart of the Pine Ridge and within striking distance of the Thousand-foot Falls, the Rio On pools and the Rio Frio Cave. The lodge has its own clear river pools. It prefers to cater to small parties but welcomes individual guests.

Hidden Valley Inn offers luxury accommodation in the Mountain Pine Ridge near the Thousand-foot Falls. Highlights include fireplaces and private baths. This lodge requires advance booking.

Warrie Head Ranch and Lodge is set in a young orange grove and on the banks of the Belize River just six miles from Belmopan, and is owned by the well-known Belizean businessman Johnny Searle and his wife, Beah. It caters mostly for inland expeditions but welcomes individual guests who book ahead. The lodge is known for its excellent bird watching and also its fine wine and food.

Banana Bank Lodge is a charming lodge located on the far side of the Belize River, and approachable by boat or car. The lady of the lodge, Carolyn Carr, is a well-known artist whose works depict Belizean life, including wildlife.

Five Sisters Falls and Lodge in the Mountain Pine Ridge. This eco-jungle lodge provides a panoramic view of the pine forest, waterfalls and granite formation. It offers accommodation in rooms or rustic cabins with thatched roofs, and has an open-air restaurant.

Blancaneaux Lodge is also in the Mountain Pine Ridge. This lodge is owned by famous film producer, Francis Ford Copolla. Italian food is the specialty here.

Hotels in Belize

In previous editions of this book we have carried information about hotels throughout the country. The rapid expansion in tourism has meant that we are unable, in fairness and accuracy, to continue this service but recommend the country-wide Hotel Guide produced and regularly updated by the Belize Tourist Board (see p.104 of this book).

The Rio On (previous page) (CUBOLA ARCHIVES)

| 12 |
General information

Geography
Belize (formerly British Honduras, until 1981) is a country of approximately 8,868 square miles, located on the east coast of Central America on the Caribbean Sea, 750 miles from Miami, Houston and New Orleans. Belize is bordered by Mexico to the north and Guatemala to the west and the south. Belize possesses the largest Barrier Reef in the Western Hemisphere (185 miles along). The land surface is flat along the coast and in the north. As you move inland, the land rises to 3,000 feet above sea-level. The vast central and southern regions of the country are covered by tropical pine, hardwood and rain forests.

Climate
The climate is sub-tropical, with a brisk prevailing wind from the Caribbean Sea. Summer highs are rarely above 95 °F, winter lows rarely below 60 °F. Annual rainfall ranges from 180 inches in the south to 60 inches in the north. The rainy season extends from May through to September with a short dry period in August.

Population
The population of Belize was approximately 230,000 in 1997, with a projected increase to 241,492 by the year 2000. This is based on an estimated growth rate of 2.6 per cent per year. It is primarily comprised of Creoles (African-European), Garifuna (African-Indian), Mestizo (Spanish-Indian), East Indian, Maya, Lebanese, Chinese and European.

Language
English is the official language and is widely spoken, as are Spanish and Creole. Maya and Garifuna are also spoken.

Government
Belize is a member of the British Commonwealth, with a democratically elected parliamentary government.

A flame tree in Belize City (M J BOURNE)

Entry requirements
Visitors are permitted to stay up to one month, provided they have a valid passport (and visa, if required). Travellers should demonstrate that they have sufficient funds for their visit (not less than US$50 per person per day) and have a ticket to their onward destination.

Visas
No visas are required from nationals of the following countries: United States, United Kingdom and Commonwealth countries, Belgium, Canada, Chile, Costa Rica, Denmark, Fiji, France, Finland, Gambia, Germany, Ghana, Greece, Guatemala, Iceland, Ireland, Italy, Luxembourg, Malawi, Mexico, Netherlands, Norway, Panama, Portugal, Spain, Suriname, Sweden, Tunisia, Turkey, Uruguay and Venezuela.

Currency
The Belize dollar (BZ$) has a fixed rate of exchange of BZ$2 to US$1. Many hotels, resorts and restaurants accept US currency, travellers cheques and credit cards.

Taxes
All passengers are required to pay a US$10 Airport Departure Tax and US$1.25 Security Tax and US$3.75 as a contribution to the Protected Areas Conservation Trust, upon departure from Belize. Hotels levy a 5 per cent Government Hotel Tax.

Electricity
The current is the same as in the United States, 110 volts a.c.

Telephone
Direct dial service is available between Belize and the United States and Canada. To dial Belize from either the United States or Canada dial 011 – 501, drop the first zero from the local city code, then dial the remaining numbers. Example:
To reach 02 – 12345, dial: 011 – 501 – 2 – 12345.
Fax and e-mail services are also available.

Time
Time observed year-round is GMT –6, which is the same as US Central Standard Time. Daylight Saving Time is not observed.

Business hours
Most banks are open Monday to Thursday 8:00 a.m. to 1:00 p.m., Friday 8:00 a.m. to 4:30 p.m. Business hours are, generally, Monday to Friday 8:00 a.m. to 12:00 p.m. and 1:00 p.m. to 5:00 p.m. Many stores are also open from 7:00 to 9:00 p.m. Many stores are closed half-days on Wednesdays and Saturdays.

Public and banking holidays
New Year's Day, January 1; Baron Bliss Day, March 9; Good Friday; Holy Saturday; Easter Sunday; Easter Monday; Labour Day, May 1; Commonwealth Day, May 24; St George's Caye Day, September 10; Independence Day, September 21; PanAmerican Day, October 12; Garifuna Settlement Day, November 19; Christmas Day, December 25; Boxing Day, December 26.

The 'Baymen' is the name given to the early settlers in Belize and given particular local emphasis by supporters of the 10th of September as Belize's greatest national holiday. This emphasis achieved political significance after the People's United Party came to power with Independence in 1981 and declared 21 September to

Fort George Hotel and the Marine Parade, Belize City (M J BOURNE)

be Belize's most important national holiday and, to a degree, discredited the 10th, which then became a rallying issue for the opposition United Democratic Party. As a result both days are now jointly acknowledged as national days and celebrations are supervised by a joint committee.

9 March, 'Baron Bliss Day', is the other important national holiday. It commemorates an eccentric English nobleman with a Portuguese title, Baron Bliss, who arrived in Belize on his yacht in 1926 to try out the fishing. He died not long afterwards, never having set foot ashore, and left a large part of his fortune to Belize in perpetual trust. A Baron Bliss Committee administers this trust and builds libraries, offers scholarships, organises art exhibitions, concerts, plays and dance recitals, and fulfills other public and social needs with the annual interest from the trust.

The Baron Bliss Memorial and lighthouse,
Marine Parade, Belize City (opposite) (M J BOURNE)

What to wear
Light, informal clothing is recommended, except for jungle excursions where the thick forest growth and insects should be taken into account. It is advisable to bring insect repellent and sun protection.

Water
Water is drinkable in towns and resort areas.

Postal rates
Postal rates to the US are BZ$0.60 for letters and BZ$0.30 for postcards. Postal rates for Europe are BZ$0.75 for letters and BZ$0.40 for postcards.

Taxis
Recognisable by their green license plates, taxis are available in towns and resort areas. They are not metered, but charge standard fares (per person).

Health
There are no endemic diseases. No inoculations are required for entry, but anti-malaria tablets are recommended for extended stays in the jungle.

Hospitals
Medical care is available at private and government hospitals and clinics throughout the country. The major hospitals in each district are listed below with their telephone numbers:
Belize City Hospital
Belize City, Tel: 02 – 77251.
Karl Heusner Memorial Hospital
Belize City, Tel: 02 – 31548.
Belmopan Public Hospital
Belmopan, Tel: 08 – 22263.
Corozal Hospital
Santa Rita Hill, Corozal Tel: 04 – 22076.
Dangriga Hospital
Dangriga, Tel: 05-22078.
Doctor's Quarters
Dangriga, Tel: 05 – 22085.

North Front Street, Belize City (M J BOURNE)

Punta Gorda Hospital
Punta Gorda, Tel: 07 – 22026.
San Ignacio Hospital
San Ignacio, Cayo, Tel 092 – 2066.

Emergency numbers

To reach the police department dial 911, and to reach the fire department or ambulance service in an emergency, dial 90.

Information service

a) United States and Canada

Belize Tourist Board
421 Seventh Avenue, New York, NY 10001
Toll Free from Continental US & Canada:
800 – 624 – 0686/(212) 563 – 6011;
Fax: (212) 563 – 6033

Belize Embassy
2535 Massachusetts Ave. NW,
Washington, DC 20008,
Tel: (202) 332 – 9636

Belize Mission to the United Nations
820 Second Avenue, New York, NY 10017
Tel: (212) 599 – 0233

Consulate of Belize (Canada)
Royal Bank Plaza
Suite 3800, South Tower
Toronto, Ontario, Canada, M5J 2J3
Tel: (416) 865 – 7000

b) Belize

Belize Tourism Board
Level Two, Central Bank Building
Belize City
Tel: (501) 2 – 31913   Fax: (501) 2 – 31943

Belize Tourism Industry Association
10 North Park Street
P.O. Box 62, Belize City
Tel: 02 – 75717

c) Europe

Belize Tourist Board
Bopserwaldstr. 40G, D-70184,
Stuttgart, Germany
Tel: (49-711) 233947

Information on Belize is also available from various web sites.

MACMILLAN CARIBBEAN GUIDES
Titles available

Anguilla: Tranquil Isle of the Caribbean – Carty and Petty
Antigua and Barbuda: The Heart of the Caribbean – Dyde
The Bahamas: A Family of Islands – Saunders
Barbados: The Visitor's Guide – Hoyos
The Islands of Bermuda: Another World – Raine
Belize: Ecotourism in Action – Cutlack
Cuba Guide – Gravette
Dominica: Isle of Adventure – Honychurch
Grenada: Isle of Spice – Sinclair
Jamaica: The Fairest Isle: A Visitor's Guide – Sherlock and Preston
Montserrat: Emerald Isle of the Caribbean – Fergus
Nevis: Queen of the Caribees – Gordon
St Kitts: Cradle of the Caribbean – Dyde
St Lucia: Helen of the West Indies – Ellis
St Vincent and the Grenadines – Sutty
The Turks and Caicos Islands: Lands of Discovery – Smithers
USVI: America's Virgin Islands – Martel